The Official Story of The Championships

WIMBLEDON
2015

WIMBLEDON AWAITS

WIMBLEDON.COM
#WIMBLEDON

The Official Story of The Championships
WIMBLEDON
2015

By Paul Newman

(Left) The official 2015 Championships poster was designed by Russian paper artist Yulia Brodskaya

VSP

Published in 2015 by Vision Sports Publishing Ltd

Vision Sports Publishing Ltd
19-23 High Street, Kingston upon Thames
Surrey, KT1 1LL
www.visionsp.co.uk

ISBN: 978-1909534-39-1

© The All England Lawn Tennis Club (Championships) Limited ('AELTC')

Written by: Paul Newman
Additional writing by: Ian Chadband
Edited by: Jim Drewett and Alexandra Willis
Production editor: Paul Baillie-Lane
Designed by: Neal Cobourne
Photography: Bob Martin, Thomas Lovelock, Roger Allen, Dillon Bryden, Jon Buckle, Florian Eisele, Javier Garcia, Eddie Keogh, Jed Leicester, David Levenson, Steve Lewis, Chris Raphael, Karwai Tang and Joe Toth
Picture research: Paul Weaver, Neil Turner and Sarah Frandsen

All photographs © AELTC

Results and tables are reproduced courtesy of the AELTC

The All England Lawn Tennis Club (Championships) Limited
Church Road, Wimbledon, London, SW19 5AE, England
Tel: +44 (0)20 8944 1066
Fax: +44 (0)20 8947 8752
www.wimbledon.com

Printed in Slovakia by Neografia

This book is reproduced with the assistance of Rolex.

CONTENTS

FOREWORD
By Philip Brook
Chairman of The All England Lawn Tennis & Croquet Club and
Committee of Management of The Championships

The Championships 2015 will be remembered for many things. New tournament dates, fabulous weather, beautiful grounds and stunning new facilities. But above all, this Championships will be remembered for the tennis. Two weeks of truly outstanding competition, every match a gladiatorial battle, every match ending in triumph for one player (or pair) and disaster for the other.

We congratulate Novak Djokovic on winning the Gentlemen's Singles Championship for the third time, defeating Roger Federer in a repeat of last year's final. Congratulations also to Serena Williams for winning her sixth Wimbledon Ladies' Singles Championship and 21st Grand Slam title, defeating Spain's up and coming Garbine Muguruza over two close sets. And to Martina Hingis, Ladies' Doubles Champion in 1996 at the age of 15, winning her third Ladies' Doubles title 19 years later and also her first Mixed Doubles title.

And there was British success – Jamie Murray reaching the Gentlemen's Doubles final, Andy the Gentlemen's Singles semi-final, and Heather Watson for playing the match of her life against Serena Williams. Jordanne Whiley retained her Wheelchair Ladies' Doubles title, a worthy accompaniment to the announcement that from next year, Gentlemen's and Ladies' Wheelchair Singles will be played at Wimbledon.

This was also the year we said goodbye to 2002 Champion Lleyton Hewitt after a Wimbledon career spanning 17 years. It was fitting that of the four matches Lleyton played this year, three of them went to five sets as once again he displayed his trademark fighting spirit, tenacity and will to win.

This year The Championships were held one week later in the calendar which meant that the players had three full weeks after the end of Roland Garros to recover from the French Open and to prepare thoroughly on grass before Wimbledon. The change in dates has been very well received, with new tour level grass court tournaments in Nottingham and Stuttgart, new Challenger level tournaments in Manchester, Surbiton and Ilkley, and excellent player fields at Queen's, Edgbaston and Eastbourne. There is more work for us to do to refine and further improve the calendar in the lead up to The Championships, but we are delighted that the principle of a three-week grass court 'swing' has been established and was so successful in its first year of operation.

I hope this annual will bring back many happy memories of Wimbledon 2015.

Philip Brook

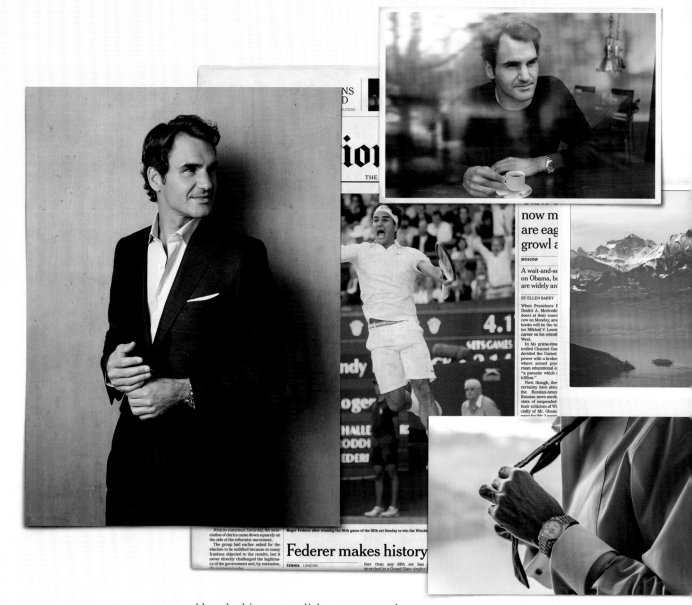

Already, his accomplishments exceed
more than most will manage in a lifetime.
He has set the mark for Grand Slam victories,
spent more weeks at number one than any other,
and secured his place as one of the game's all-time best.
And now he's embarked on yet another journey:
to help provide a quality education for hundreds of
thousands of underprivileged children in Southern Africa.
But no matter what challenge he chooses
to undertake, his Rolex is always with him,
marking the moments he will always remember,
and the achievements still to come.

INTRODUCTION
By Paul Newman

They were words that might have struck fear into some of Roger Federer's rivals. "It's probably been the best preparation I've ever had for Wimbledon," the Swiss said two days before the start of The Championships. "The game's good. I've been playing well for a year now. It's been a good last week as well in Halle. Practice has been good. So the body's fine, too." The main reason for the seven-times Gentlemen's Singles Champion's optimism? "We have had a week more on the grass," he said. "I'm sure I'm not the only one saying that this year."

The Championships 2015 was to prove memorable for many reasons, but one of the most significant was its new place in the calendar. Ever since 1911 the Wimbledon Fortnight had started six weeks before the first Monday in August, which in turn meant that the French Open finished only two weeks before the start of The Championships. The short gap between the end of the clay court campaign and the start of The Championships had given players little time to find their feet on grass. Some felt they had to choose between the two events. Manuel Santana, the French Open champion of 1961 and 1964, skipped Roland Garros in 1966 and instead came to Britain for five weeks to prepare – successfully – for The Championships. Ivan Lendl was another who missed Paris in order to improve his chances at the All England Club, though he never achieved his goal of lifting the Challenge Cup on Centre Court.

For years there had been talk of lengthening the grass court season and in 2012 Philip Brook, the Chairman of the All England Club, announced that from 2015 The Championships would start a week later in order to give players more time to recuperate after the French Open and to hone their grass court game.

The benefits of the change were soon evident, especially among those who had gone deep into the French Open. Stan Wawrinka, the men's champion at Roland Garros, had time to rest for four days at home in Switzerland, practise for three days on grass at The Queen's Club, compete in the Aegon Championships and then have another week of grass court preparation.

The biggest grass court events before The Championships – at Queen's Club and Halle for the men and at Edgbaston and Eastbourne for the women – all moved back a week, which gave players the chance to compete in their usual build-up tournaments and have the extra week's rest. Federer and Andy Murray took it easy for a few days before competing at Halle and Queen's Club respectively, where the benefits of the new arrangements were evident as they won the tournaments. The extra chances to rest and practise were also welcomed by those who generally choose not to compete anywhere before The Championships. Serena Williams and Novak Djokovic both opted again for practice courts rather than competition courts; by the end of the Wimbledon Fortnight it would be clear how well their preparations had gone.

For others the three-week gap offered the opportunity to play more competitive matches on grass. Rafael Nadal won the new grass court tournament in Stuttgart in the week immediately following the French Open and went into The Championships having already played five matches on grass, which was the most since he won his first Wimbledon title in 2008. In the same week, Nicolas Mahut and Camila Giorgi won at 's-Hertogenbosch. In the week before The Championships Denis Istomin beat Sam Querrey in the Nottingham final, and 18-year-old Belinda Bencic became the youngest player since 2008 to win a Premier-level trophy on the women's tour when she beat Agnieszka Radwanska in the final at Eastbourne.

And so to the All England Club, where the start on Monday 29th June was the latest since the 13th July start in 1896. The Gentlemen's Singles Champion that year was Edinburgh-born Harold Maloney. Might that be an omen for Scotland's Andy Murray? We would soon find out.

HANGING OUT IN SW19

Wimbledon is always a bit fevered in the build-up to The Championships but the additional week for players to prepare following the French Open ensured an unusually relaxed ambience around the Grounds as players arrived earlier than usual to prepare. The extra time offered them more chance to shoot the breeze (and hoops), to enjoy a few laughs, to high five the occasional young fan and, in Novak Djokovic's case, to potter around SW19 on his push bike. Basically, the chill before the furnace…

WIMBLEDON 2015
Gentlemen's Singles Seeds

 Novak DJOKOVIC ❶
(Serbia)
Age: 28

| Wimbledon titles: 2 | Grand Slam titles: 8 |

 Roger FEDERER ❷
(Switzerland)
Age: 33

| Wimbledon titles: 7 | Grand Slam titles: 17 |

 Andy MURRAY ❸
(Great Britain)
Age: 28

| Wimbledon titles: 1 | Grand Slam titles: 2 |

Stan WAWRINKA ❹
(Switzerland)
Age: 30

| Wimbledon titles: 0 | Grand Slam titles: 2 |

 Kei NISHIKORI ❺
(Japan)
Age: 25

| Wimbledon titles: 0 | Grand Slam titles: 0 |

 Tomas BERDYCH ❻
(Czech Republic)
Age: 29

| Wimbledon titles: 0 | Grand Slam titles: 0 |

 Milos RAONIC ❼
(Canada)
Age: 24

| Wimbledon titles: 0 | Grand Slam titles: 0 |

 David FERRER ❽
(Spain)
Age: 33 WITHDRAWN

| Wimbledon titles: 0 | Grand Slam titles: 0 |

Marin CILIC (Croatia) ❾

Rafael NADAL (Spain) ❿

Grigor DIMITROV (Bulgaria) ⓫

Gilles SIMON (France) ⓬

Jo-Wilfried TSONGA (France) ⓭

Kevin ANDERSON (South Africa) ⓮

Feliciano LOPEZ (Spain) ⓯

David GOFFIN (Belgium) ⓰

Ladies' Singles Seeds

Serena WILLIAMS ❶
(USA)
Age: 33

Wimbledon titles: 5 | Grand Slam titles: 20

Petra KVITOVA ❷
(Czech Republic)
Age: 25

Wimbledon titles: 2 | Grand Slam titles: 2

Simona HALEP ❸
(Romania)
Age: 23

Wimbledon titles: 0 | Grand Slam titles: 0

Maria SHARAPOVA ❹
(Russia)
Age: 28

Wimbledon titles: 1 | Grand Slam titles: 5

Caroline WOZNIACKI ❺
(Denmark)
Age: 24

Wimbledon titles: 0 | Grand Slam titles: 0

Lucie SAFAROVA ❻
(Czech Republic)
Age: 28

Wimbledon titles: 0 | Grand Slam titles: 0

Ana IVANOVIC ❼
(Serbia)
Age: 27

Wimbledon titles: 0 | Grand Slam titles: 0

Ekaterina MAKAROVA ❽
(Russia)
Age: 27

Wimbledon titles: 0 | Grand Slam titles: 0

Carla SUAREZ NAVARRO (Spain) ❾

AGNIESZKA RADWANSKA (Poland) ⑬

Angelique KERBER (Germany) ❿

ANDREA PETKOVIC (Germany) ⑭

KAROLINA PLISKOVA (Czech Republic) ⑪

TIMEA BACSINSZKY (Switzerland) ⑮

EUGENIE BOUCHARD (Canada) ⑫

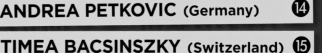

VENUS WILLIAMS (USA) ⑯

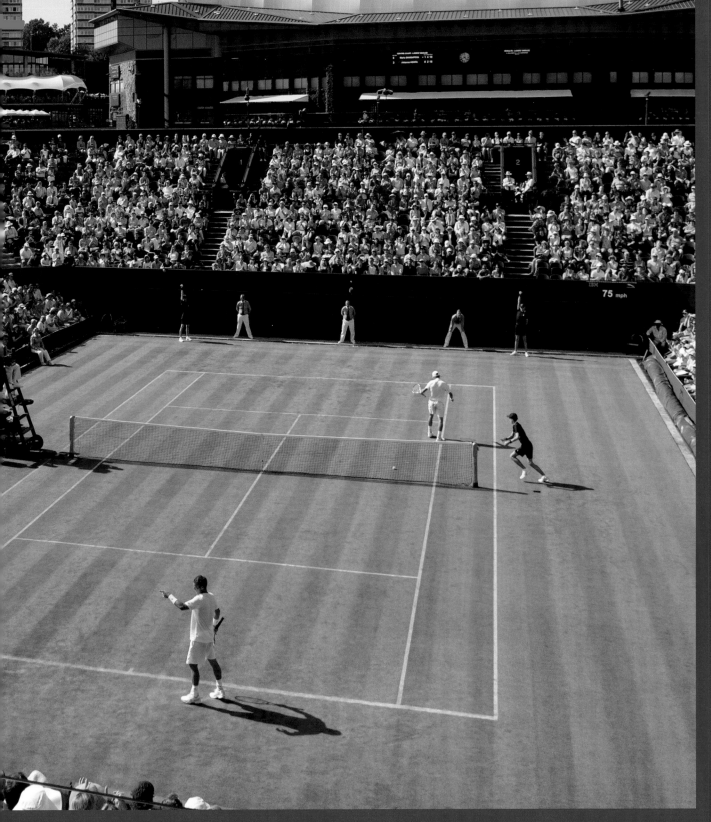

DAY ONE
MONDAY 29 JUNE

I f you ask those who have been attending The Championships for more years than they care to remember what the weather used to be like, you can expect most of their replies to be on similar lines: occasionally a little chilly in the first week, with a fair chance of some rain, but nearly always better in the second as the temperatures rise in line with the excitement. With The Championships moving back a week in the calendar there was always the likelihood that the Wimbledon Fortnight would be blessed with good weather in 2015, and the opening day lived up to all expectations. The sun shone brightly on a glorious English summer's day as the 129th edition of The Championships got under way.

Crowds gather around the southern courts (above) to watch the opening day of The Championships 2015

Since 1934 it has been the tradition that the Gentlemen's Singles Champion from the previous year opens proceedings on Centre Court. Twelve months after his thrilling victory over Roger Federer in the 2014 final, it was the turn of Novak Djokovic to begin play in the most famous arena in tennis. The draw had given him, in theory, the most difficult start possible in that his opponent, Philipp Kohlschreiber, was ranked No.33 in the world. The German was the highest-ranked player in the men's field not to be seeded.

Nevertheless, there were plenty of reasons for Djokovic to feel confident, even if his last competitive appearance had seen him lose to Stan Wawrinka in the final of the French Open, which remains the one jewel missing from his Grand Slam crown. Djokovic had returned to No.1 in the world rankings with his second triumph at The Championships in 2014 and had stayed there ever since.

For all the continued brilliance of Roger Federer, the resurgence of Andy Murray and Wawrinka's extended Indian summer, there could be no argument about the identity of the world's best player. Since October 2014 Djokovic had played in eight tournaments at ATP Masters 1000 level or higher and won seven of them, his only defeat coming in the final at Roland Garros. At 28, he was in his prime.

Djokovic made a few more unforced errors than usual, particularly in the early stages, but never looked in any serious trouble as he eased to a 6-4, 6-4, 6-4 victory. There was a neat symmetry about the match, with Djokovic breaking serve in the 10th game of all three sets. Asked afterwards if he had felt any rustiness in his game, Djokovic said: "Not much." He said it had been "a great performance against a quality opponent". The result certainly pleased one of Djokovic's fans, Stella Riley, who had arrived two days earlier at 7.30am to take first place in the Queue, a full day before it had officially opened.

Just as he had in his pre-Championships press conference the previous day, Djokovic was asked questions about his coach Boris Becker's comments concerning on-court communications. The Grand Slam Rule Book states that coaches and players must not communicate during a match, but Becker had told BBC Radio 5 Live: "There are moments when he looks up and he needs assurance that what he is doing is right. And then we have our ways about it to tell him it's good or tell him it's bad. And then it's up to him to change it."

Djokovic, however, insisted again that he was not being given on-court coaching. He explained: "There are certain ways of communication which is encouragement, which is support, which is understanding the moment when to clap or say something that can lift my energy up, that can motivate me to play a certain point. But it's all within the rules. If I am breaking any rules, or my team are, I would be fined."

The draw had offered the mouth-watering prospect of a second-round meeting between Djokovic and Lleyton Hewitt, the 2002 champion, but if that had been in the script then somebody forgot to tell Jarkko Nieminen. Hewitt, making his final bow at The Championships before he retires after his 20th consecutive appearance at the Australian Open next year, was beaten 6-3, 3-6, 6-4, 0-6, 9-11 by the Finn on No.2 Court after a typically dramatic contest that lasted four hours. It was the 56th time that Hewitt had played a Grand Slam match that had gone to five sets.

(Left) Ground capacity had been increased to 39,000, which made St Mary's Walk a busy place to be

Defending champion Novak Djokovic was first to play on Centre Court

FAREWELL
TO A LEGEND

One by one, the effusive tributes poured in from his fellow players to mark the last singles hurrah of Lleyton Hewitt. "Never the strongest or the tallest but with the spirit of a champion," said Maria Sharapova. "One of the greatest competitors we had in sport," declared Novak Djokovic.

"He was the first guy really from the baseline to have a major impact and he showed an entire generation how it can be done," was Roger Federer's verdict on his old sparring partner, the 2002 Wimbledon champ.

Yet beyond all these plaudits following Hewitt's defeat by Jarkko Nieminen – his ninth five-set thriller in 17 Wimbledon singles campaigns – lay the most heartfelt of all, from the yellow-shirted devotees who have spent a fortune travelling around the world down the years to follow and pay homage to their beloved 'Rusty'.

Gareth Fletcher, chief cheerleader of the Fanatics who gave him such a rousing send off on No.2 Court, wasn't about to

cry when he knew his teak-tough hero wouldn't shed tears either.

"If you could pick a way for him to go out, you'd say saving match points and losing 11-9 in the fifth was fitting," said Gareth, who was once a ball boy in a Hewitt match 17 years ago and has been following the little bloke with the big heart ever since. With his mates, he had flown from Brisbane to London to watch his idol one last time at Wimbledon.

But why Hewitt, whose best days had long disappeared, and not the exciting new brigade like Nick Kyrgios and Bernie Tomic? Gareth looked aghast at the question. "Because of his attitude, his passion, his refusal to accept any cause was a lost one," he said.

"People love him because whatever's happening in a match, he keeps fighting, never says die – and to me, he's almost the definition of a true, blue Australian, the epitome of Aussie spirit. That's why we follow him and people love him. There'll never be another like Lleyton Hewitt...."

Hewitt said afterwards: "That pretty much sums up my career, I guess: my mentality, going out there, my never-say-die attitude. I've lived for that the 18, 19 years I've been on tour. As I tell people, it's not something I work at. I'm fortunate that I have a lot of self-motivation to go out there and get the most out of myself, whether it's in the gym, behind the scenes, whatever. Obviously I'm proud of myself that I went out there and left it all out."

In his long career, which has been interrupted by a series of injuries in his latter years, Hewitt reached No.1 in the world rankings and won Wimbledon, the US Open and the Davis Cup. However, there was no doubt about the highlight, which the 34-year-old Australian was able to contemplate on the eve of The Championships as he spent some time sitting on his own in an empty Centre Court.

"I was thinking about that walk you do, the tradition of the tournament, playing on Centre Court," he said. "For me, it's the home of tennis. I don't get the same feeling walking into any other grounds in the world – no other tennis court, no other complex – that I do here. I do get goosebumps walking into this place. I'm so fortunate. One of the greatest things about winning this Championship is becoming a member of it [the Club]. For me to be able to go in the Members' locker room four weeks before Wimbledon with some of the older members, sit down and have a cup of tea and a chat, it's a lot of fun. That's something I can always come back and enjoy over the years."

The previous match on No.2 Court had featured an Australian from the other end of the age scale. Nick Kyrgios, who made an indelible mark on his debut at The Championships by reaching last year's quarter-finals at the expense of Rafael Nadal, sometimes makes as many headlines for his behaviour as he does for his tennis, and his 6-0, 6-2, 7-6(6) victory over Diego Schwartzman was no exception. The colourful 20-year-old from Canberra was two sets up when he had an angry confrontation with Mohamed Lahyani, the umpire, about a contentious line call.

No.2 Court rises to acclaim Jarkko Nieminen, the final conqueror of Wimbledon legend Lleyton Hewitt

WIMBLEDON IN NUMBERS

24 Years since a man aged 37 won a first round singles match at The Championships, Tommy Haas taking over from Jimmy Connors

Tempers seemed to rise with the temperatures. Serena Williams was given a code violation for an "audible obscenity" following a nasty fall during her 6-4, 6-1 victory over Russia's Margarita Gasparyan, as was Liam Broady, who gave the host country its first victory when he came back from two sets down on his senior debut at The Championships to beat Australia's Marinko Matosevic 5-7, 4-6, 6-3, 6-2, 6-3. "I think it's a $2,500 fine," he said afterwards. "I wouldn't have sworn if I'd known how much it was!" The win guaranteed Broady a pay cheque of £47,000, which was only £16,000 less than he had earned in his entire career. The 21-year-old from Stockport was ranked No.473 in the world at the start of 2014, but climbed into the top 200 after some good results at Challenger level.

With Naomi Broady also given a wild card, a British brother and sister played in the main draw for the first time since Linda and Buster Mottram in 1978. However, Naomi was beaten 6-7(5), 3-6 by Colombia's Mariana Duque-Marino. Jo Konta, the British No.2, "enjoyed every minute" of her Centre Court debut against Maria Sharapova but was beaten 2-6, 2-6. Heather Watson, the British No.1, was involved in late-evening drama when her meeting with France's Caroline Garcia was suspended just after 9pm because of bad light with the score at one set apiece.

Naomi Broady (below) and Liam Broady (below right) became the first British brother and sister to compete in the main draw at Wimbledon since 1978

Kei Nishikori nursed a sore calf strain through five sets before beating Simone Bolelli 6-3, 6-7(4), 6-2, 3-6, 6-3, while Wawrinka eased past Portugal's Joao Sousa, winning 6-2, 7-5, 7-6(3). Andrea Petkovic and Venus Williams completed the first 6-0, 6-0 "double bagels" at The Championships for six years, beating Shelby Rogers and Madison Brengle respectively, while 37-year-old Tommy Haas struck a blow for the older generation following his return from yet another prolonged absence through injury. In beating Dusan Lajovic 6-2, 6-3, 4-6, 6-2, Haas became the oldest man to win a singles match at The Championships since 38-year-old Jimmy Connors beat Veli Paloheimo and Aaron Krickstein in 1991.

115 mph

Novak's Feathered Friend

• **When you are setting out** on the defence of your Gentlemen's Singles Championship, any moral support is welcome. So after Novak Djokovic's unexpected new number one fan had fluttered on to take up Centre Court residence as he prepared to serve against Philipp Kohlschreiber, the Serb said that he was convinced the "sparrow bird from Belgrade" had flown a thousand miles to support him.

"Yeah, the bird didn't want to go away, it just loves tennis, I guess," chuckled the champion, recalling how the blue tit – Djoko's tennis is better than his ornithology, evidently – eventually had to be ushered gently away from the court by a ball boy.

So how did Rufus the Hawk, whose job is to warn off little invaders like Djokovic's new friend, fail in his duty? Wimbledon's original avian superstar Rufus just tweeted with a sniff on his personal Twitter feed: "My domain is pigeons. I think he's just after my autograph."

• **Howzat!** The All England Club chairman Philip Brook jumped nobly into action when a wayward stroke arrowed alarmingly towards the Royal Box in which he was sitting. "With the ball heading straight for one of our Royal Box guests, Fiona Bruce, I knew a good catch was required," smiled the Chairman, who plucked the ball out the air to protect the popular presenter of the BBC's *Antiques Roadshow*.

• **Thanasi Kokkinakis**, the young Australian hope, had been ill in the week leading up to his first round defeat by Leonardo Mayer. "I'm still finding out what antibiotics I'm about to take. I'll get the results today," he said, before adding wryly: "Which is helpful now that I'm out!"

Serena Williams holds forth on her preparations for The Championships

• **There are different** ways of preparing for the rigours of The Fortnight but nobody quite has the unique style of Serena Williams. Two days before beating her first-round opponent, Margarita Gasparyan, the five-times champion was talked into going on stage with pop superstar Taylor Swift in front of 65,000 cheering fans.

"I was really nervous. I didn't really want to do it," she explained, before being asked if she fancied a post-tennis musical career. "Yes. But the problem is I don't have a voice, so I don't have a choice," she laughed, as her pal Drake, the rapper, sat at the back of the main interview room chuckling.

• **For every player**, a new Wimbledon always begins at love-all, so how appropriate that Neal Skupski, the British professional who teamed up with brother Ken in the Gentlemen's Doubles, should start the Fortnight by announcing on social media his engagement to girlfriend Cambri Prevost, accompanied by a picture of the "future Mr and Mrs Skupski" celebrating on The Hill.

DELI

COFFEE

EVERY PLAYER A WINNER

Wimbledon's reputation as the Grand Slam at which only the best will do for its players was enhanced by the creation of advanced new facilities and services in 2015. From the new underground stretching, warm-up and physiotherapy area and expanded player lounge in the Millennium Building to the completely renovated Aorangi Pavilion, now entirely dedicated to players' needs with its new dressing rooms, lounge, restaurant and improved creche facilities, everything was geared to making the Wimbledon experience even cooler.

AORANGI PAVILION

Laundry

Please return
neoprene socks to
the hooks

DAY TWO

TUESDAY 30 JUNE

O n a day when the temperature on Centre Court topped 41C, one Wimbledon favourite wilted in the heat while home hopes blossomed. Four British men reached the second round for the first time in nine years and Heather Watson recovered to win from match point down, but Eugenie Bouchard's disappointing year took another unwelcome turn when she was beaten by an opponent ranked No.117 in the world.

Andy Murray (right) celebrated a relatively straightforward first round win

With the temperature rising, the All England Club decided to cut the ground capacity to around 38,000 because of concerns about a lack of shade and access to water for some spectators. More than 43,000 in total had come through the gates on the first day.

With the glorious exception of Andy Murray, The Championships have not been a happy hunting ground for British men ever since Tim Henman reached the last of his eight quarter-finals in 2004. Whether it has been down to the pressure on home players, unlucky draws or simply a shortage of talent, Murray has repeatedly been left to fly the flag on his own. Even a brief flurry of success in 2006 did not last long: after Murray, Henman, Richard Bloomfield, Jamie Delgado and Martin Lee all reached the second round, only Murray went further.

Nevertheless, Liam Broady's victory on the first day had raised British spirits and by the end of the second day Murray, James Ward and Aljaz Bedene had joined him in the second round. Murray beat Mikhail Kukushkin 6-4, 7-6(3), 6-4, Ward defeated Luca Vanni 6-7(4), 6-2, 6-4, 6-3 and Bedene fought back to beat Radek Stepanek 7-5, 1-6, 4-6, 6-3, 6-4.

Murray's passage was not as smooth as the scoreline might have suggested. Kukushkin, who had taken a set off Rafael Nadal the previous year, went for broke from the start. His thumping ground strokes, hit low and flat over the net, had little margin for error but were highly effective and Murray was unable to dictate the rallies as he would have liked. However, apart from some anxious moments in the second set the world No.3 never looked in any real danger.

"The way he played just made it extremely difficult to play offensive tennis," Murray said afterwards, clutching a sheet of post-match statistics. "Sometimes you just have to knuckle down and try to get the win. It doesn't say on this match report how well I played, it just says that I won the match. That's the most important thing."

Aljaz Bedene came through against Radek Stepanek in five sets

Ward had been drawn to play David Ferrer in the first round, but the world No.7's late withdrawal because of injury left the Briton facing a 30-year-old Italian making his Wimbledon debut. Ward's big-match experience and grass court expertise proved decisive. The 28-year-old Briton had been knocking on the door of the world's top 100 since the end of 2014 and had confirmed his ability to rise to the occasion with his crucial Davis Cup victory in March over John Isner. Vanni, a lucky loser from the final round of qualifying, had some success with his big serve in the opening set before Ward took control.

James Ward reproduced his Davis Cup form to reach the second round

Bedene, meanwhile, enjoyed his first victory at The Championships as a home player. The world No.75 was born in Slovenia but has been based in Hertfordshire since 2008 and was granted British citizenship in March. His fiancée, a singer whose stage name is Kimalie, used to be a member of Slovenia's equivalent of the Spice Girls and now works closely with the musician and tennis fan, Jeff Wayne, of *War of the Worlds* fame. Bedene revealed another connection with show business when he talked about the house where they were staying not far from the All England Club. "The lady who runs the house is an actress, Tessa Wyatt," he said. "She was married to a famous DJ back in the 1970s. I think was his name was Tony Blackburn."

Stepanek, a former world No.8, was a tricky opponent, but Bedene benefited from some pre-match tips from Murray to record an emotional victory. "I got tears in my eyes and usually this does not happen," he said after the match. "I tried to stay focused for the last game and when I won, it just came out of me. I went a little bit squeaky-voiced."

Kyle Edmund and Brydan Klein, beaten by Alexandr Dolgopolov and Andreas Seppi respectively, were unable to add further chapters to the story of British success, but it

WHERE DID YOU GET THAT HAT?

When the going gets hot, the Brits get inventive. The most important accoutrement for anyone attending this most sweltering of Wimbledons was, naturally, a decent hat – and it didn't have to be that cool to keep you cool. If you didn't have a Panama or some floppy, flowery headgear, a copy of your morning paper would do. Though, of course, in the fashion stakes, you could trust Roger Federer's legion of Swiss fans **(right)** to always look the part...

WIMBLEDON IN NUMBERS

2

Matches won by Eugenie Bouchard, last year's singles finalist, out of her last 14

was still a good day for the British men. "I think everyone's picked their game up," Ward said. "Everyone's been playing well coming into the tournament. Everyone's ranking is improving. It's good to have a few more guys playing well and winning matches."

The host nation had less success in the Ladies' Singles Championship, with Watson the only Briton to make the second round. The 23-year-old from Guernsey emerged with great credit from her 1-6, 6-3, 8-6 victory over France's Caroline Garcia, the No.32 seed. The match had been called off the previous evening because of bad light after the second set. When they resumed Watson had to save three match points when serving at 4-5. Having broken to go 6-5 up, she failed to serve out for victory, only to break again in the following game. At 7-6 and 40-0 Watson double-faulted, but on the next point Garcia hit a return long.

Laura Robson was cheerful despite losing in the first round

Laura Robson, Watson's predecessor as British No.1, had not played in a Grand Slam tournament since the 2014 Australian Open, but the 2008 girls' singles champion ended a 17-month absence with a wrist injury nine days before the start of The Championships in the qualifying tournament at Eastbourne. A 0-6, 1-6 defeat to Daria Gavrilova had not augured well for her chances at the All England Club, but the former world No.27 played much better, despite losing 4-6, 4-6 to Evgeniya Rodina. "I'm pretty confident that I have the ability to get back to where I was, if not higher," Robson said. "It's going to be a long process to get there, but I'm very excited that I have another chance to do it."

While Robson had missed The Championships 2014, one of her contemporaries had stolen the show. Bouchard won the crowd's affections last year with her dynamic tennis, engaging smile and tales of her family's love of British royalty. However, not much had gone right for the 21-year-old Canadian subsequently. She replaced Nick Saviano, her coach of the previous 12 years, with Sam Sumyk, who had enjoyed great success with Victoria Azarenka, but lost 11 times in 13 matches in the build-up to this year's Championships.

A 6-7(3), 4-6 defeat to Ying-Ying Duan, a big-hitting 25-year-old from China making her debut in The Championships, was no great surprise, especially as Bouchard played despite a torn abdominal muscle. "In my head, it was no question I was going to play, even though I was

*Last year's finalist Eugenie Bouchard **(left)** had her Wimbledon ended by Ying-Ying Duan*

World No.106 Jana Cepelova took down third seed Simona Halep

advised not to," she said afterwards. "It's so hard to be forced not to play tennis, especially at Wimbledon."

She added: "It's been a huge learning process to have great results and then have so much attention, then have bad results, just learning about the ups and downs of life and tennis, how things won't always go perfectly like I expect them to."

Last year's final had been the shortest for 31 years, with Petra Kvitova beating Bouchard for the loss of only three games in just 55 minutes. When the Czech began the defence of her title she started as she had left off, needing only 35 minutes to beat Kiki Bertens 6-1, 6-0. The only point Kvitova dropped on her serve was a double fault in the final game. She later joked that she would have to apologise for the speed of the match to her parents, who had come to watch but were returning home immediately afterwards.

Tomas Berdych won the last match of the day, finishing at 9.29pm in gathering darkness

Simona Halep, who lost to Bouchard in last year's semi-finals, became the highest-ranked player so far to go out when she was beaten 7-5, 4-6, 3-6 by Slovakia's Jana Cepelova, the world No.106. The No.3 seed's form had dipped in recent weeks and she lost in the second round of the French Open. "I knew it would be a difficult tournament for me, but I didn't expect to lose in the first round," said the Romanian. After Venus Williams and Andrea Petkovic had recorded the first "double bagel" victories at The Championships for six years on day one, Angelique Kerber followed suit with a 6-0, 6-0 demolition of her fellow German, Carina Witthoeft.

Roger Federer and Rafael Nadal started with quickfire victories over Damir Dzumhur and Thomaz Bellucci respectively, Jo-Wilfried Tsonga was taken to five sets by Gilles Muller, and Jack Sock, seeded at a Grand Slam tournament for the first time, was beaten 3-6, 6-3, 3-6, 3-6 by Sam Groth. The glorious weather had made it a day that you never wanted to end, but at least Tomas Berdych took advantage of every last ray of sunshine. The clock read 9.29pm when the Czech completed his 6-2, 6-7(8), 7-6(3), 7-6(5) victory over Jeremy Chardy in rapidly fading light.

Triple Double Bagel

- **Some weird, wonderful** and woeful tennis shots adorned the second day. Alexandr Dolgopolov smacked a ball into his own face when trying to pick up a half-volley against Britain's Kyle Edmund, while the ever-entertaining Gael Monfils had everyone in stitches, executing what was quickly dubbed a flying 'karate kick' backhand in his win over Pablo Carreno Busta.

Yet pride of place went to poor old Thomaz Bellucci, the Brazilian who missed the simplest smash followed by the easiest volley against Rafa Nadal, only for commentator Tim Henman to lament: "I hate to say it but I think he's hit the two worst shots at Wimbledon this year."

- **So, we don't see a 6-0 6-0 triumph** in any ladies' singles match at Wimbledon for six years and then, like buses running up Church Road, three come along almost together.

In the space of two days, Venus Williams hammered Madison Brengle, Andrea Petkovic allowed Shelby Rogers just 15 points in 39 minutes and Angelique Kerber treated Carina Witthoeft to the celebrated "double bagel" feast before offering the wonderfully charitable observation: "It was very close, actually."

- **Ever fancied the dream role** of being Wimbledon champion? The Live @ Wimbledon team put the job up for offer and recorded the applications from a few hopeful candidates.

A fellow calling himself Andrew Murray, asked to describe himself in three words, responded lugubriously, "Boring, unfunny and miserable", while admitting his weakness for the job was "chocolate".

Next up was a chap simply called "Roger" who described himself as an "offensive baseliner" whose weakness was: "I'm old!" Asked why he should be given the job, he pleaded: "Because I have the experience. Give me the chance to win one more!!"

The least convincing interviewee may have been a certain Maria Sharapova. Pressed to give a reason why she should have the job, she could only giggle: "Actually, I'm not really sure now why I applied!"

The candidates were told they would find out whether they were successful the weekend after next....

Eugenie Bouchard admitting she would be letting off steam after her first-round defeat

- **Outwardly, Eugenie Bouchard** handled her early exit with calmness and grace but what did Canada's hugely disappointed star really feel like? "I definitely wasn't going to break my racket on the court, that's for sure. You can't do that at Wimbledon," she said, before offering a warning with a smile to her SW19 neighbours: "Maybe something will explode later tonight."

CHAMPIONSHIPS
NOTEBOOK
Day 2

DAY THREE
WEDNESDAY 1 JULY

T he weather forecasters had predicted that Britain's mini heatwave would peak on the first Wednesday and they were right. The hottest day ever at The Championships saw the temperature hit 35.7C in the shade, which beat the previous record of 34.6C set in the scorching summer of 1976. Nevertheless, the All England Club was not the hottest place in town. A temperature of 36.7C was recorded at Heathrow, making it the hottest July day in London since records began. The heat made for testing conditions for spectators, on-court officials and ball boys and ball girls. A ball boy fainted during John Isner's victory over Matthew Ebden, though it was later reported that he felt much better after treatment.

Spectators surrounded the outside courts for the start of the second round

The six additional ice baths in the locker rooms were welcomed by the players, though there was barely a murmur of complaint about the on-court environment on this hottest of days. Most of the players have become accustomed to handling even more extreme weather at tournaments like the Australian Open and US Open, where high humidity can add to the difficulties. Grigor Dimitrov, who beat Steve Johnson 7-6(8), 6-2, 7-6(2), thought it was "just a normal day" and "not that warm". Novak Djokovic, who beat Jarkko Nieminen 6-4, 6-2, 6-3, said the conditions had been better than he had expected. "People were talking about it and predicting really difficult conditions, but I didn't find it as difficult as I thought it might be," he said. Isner said it had been "very hot" but added: "I do train in Florida and it's way worse in Florida than it was here today."

The player who seemed to have the greatest difficulty was Bernard Tomic, who earned a third-round meeting with Djokovic by beating Pierre-Hugues Herbert 7-6(3), 6-4, 7-6(5). Tomic complained of dizziness, though he also said he had had trouble sleeping. "I was fatigued and starting to get dizzy out there with the heat hitting me," he said. "It was tough, so I had to slow things down. I had to catch my breath. Hopefully I can get a good night's sleep in tonight. I just haven't been sleeping well here. It's been too hot."

In such surroundings it was perhaps no surprise that the two biggest upsets of the day saw Americans knock out Europeans. Bethanie Mattek-Sands beat Ana Ivanovic, the No.7 seed and a former semi-finalist, 6-3, 6-4, while Coco Vandeweghe beat Karolina Pliskova, the No.11 seed, 7-6(5), 6-4.

Mattek-Sands is the most adventurous dresser on the women's tour; she was also believed to be the only player pictured on the WTA website's official profile pages with bright blue and green hair. The All England Club's "almost entirely white" decree on clothing might have cramped her style, but with her knee-length socks, floral tattoos and a hint of pink and purple in her hair she was still instantly recognisable out

Former quarter-finalist Bernard Tomic admitted struggling on the hottest day of the year

on No.3 Court. Her tennis was equally impressive. The 30-year-old American had won the doubles titles at the Australian and French Opens in partnership with Lucie Safarova and the benefits of her doubles expertise were clear. Playing an aggressive serve-and-volley game, Mattek-Sands repeatedly forced errors from Ivanovic, who was being cheered from the sidelines by the German international and Manchester United-bound footballer, Bastian Schweinsteiger. It was as if Mattek-Sands was determined to make up for lost time after missing The Championships 2014 because of a hip injury. Having slipped to No.158 in the world rankings, she had to win three matches in qualifying just to make the main draw this year.

Mattek-Sands said that she had been determined to keep Ivanovic on the back foot. "She likes to play aggressive and she likes that run-around forehand and she wants to be dictating the points," Mattek-Sands said. "I really went out there trying to be the first one to do that. I was playing aggressive. I was going to throw in slices and throw in some serve-and-volleys, and really play aggressive and work my way to the net. That's grass court tennis, but that's how I play on all the surfaces. That's how I played on clay and it's how I play here. I felt like I was able to dictate the points a lot today and really make her feel rushed."

Vandeweghe also showed how power and aggression can reap a major dividend on grass. The 23-year-old New Yorker hit 15 aces and 32 winners in beating Pliskova, who has a big serve of her own and had been one of the players of the year so far, reaching the finals in Sydney, Dubai and Edgbaston, and winning the title in Prague.

The only American woman to lose in singles was Lauren Davis, who was beaten 4-6, 4-6 by her compatriot, Sloane Stephens. The Williams sisters stayed on course for a fourth-round showdown by

Qualifier Bethanie Mattek-Sands (left) beat Ana Ivanovic by playing her own game

HOT HOT HOT!

So how do you cope with the hottest day in recorded Wimbledon annals? Well, if you were a spectator you could get fanned by flapping towels on The Hill, turn your magazine into a shelter or be offered a refreshing spray from a friend. If you were a player, you could, like Nick Kyrgios, douse your head with a bottle of water. Yet even if on occasion, you felt as uncomfortable as Stan Wawrinka looked, this historically sunny afternoon still had to be worth a broad smile.

29 Out of 38 points won by Bethanie Mattek-Sands at the net during her straight sets upset of Ana Ivanovic

recording straight-sets victories in the second round. Serena beat Hungary's Timea Babos 6-4, 6-1 in just 59 minutes, while Venus faced sterner opposition from Yulia Putintseva of Kazakhstan, but still won 7-6(5), 6-4.

Serena's victory earned her a third-round meeting with Heather Watson, who enjoyed a resounding 6-4, 6-2 victory over Daniela Hantuchova, a former world No.5. From 3-1 down in the first set Watson won 11 of the last 14 games. As is her custom, Watson chased down balls to all corners of the court, but there was more to the British No.1's game than her athleticism. She packed a powerful punch when she went for winners and also showed a fine touch with some of her drop shots.

Liam Broady, Watson's fellow Briton, went out of the Gentlemen's Singles Championship, losing 6-7(3), 1-6, 1-6 in the second round to David Goffin, the No.16 seed from Belgium. Broady, who was making his debut at The Championships, said: "He was just so solid for the whole match. He knew when to apply pressure and when to soak it up. I tried to fight until the end. Sometimes it's tough because against these guys, if your legs are slightly tired or you are slightly off on the day, they take advantage of it. And that's what happened."

The temperature can usually be guaranteed to rise when Nick Kyrgios is on court and the Australian got in hot water with officials during his 7-6(5), 6-3, 6-4 victory over Juan Monaco. A line judge reported Kyrgios to the umpire, Ali Nili, after the No.26 seed swore when he lost a point towards the end of the first set. Kyrgios subsequently confronted the umpire and was heard to ask him: "Does it feel good to be up there in that chair? Does it make you feel strong?"

Marin Cilic, the US Open champion, had a narrow escape against Ricardas Berankis before winning 6-3, 4-6, 7-6(6), 4-6, 7-5. Berankis failed to convert two break points at 5-5 in the deciding set and in the following game served a double fault when match point down. Stan Wawrinka, the French Open champion, had fewer problems against Victor Estrella Burgos and won 6-3, 6-4, 7-5.

Nick Kyrgios kept his Wimbledon dreams alive (opposite page) *while Marin Cilic survived several spanners thrown by Ricardas Berankis* (below)

Kei Nishikori, the No.5 seed, pulled out of The Championships before his second-round match because of a calf strain which he had been carrying since the Halle tournament in June. Tommy Haas, who at 37 had become the oldest man to win a match at Wimbledon since 1991 with his first-round victory, came close to taking Milos Raonic to five sets before losing 0-6, 2-6, 7-6(5), 6-7(4).

Martina Hingis and Sania Mirza, the top seeds in the Ladies' Doubles Championship, got off to a winning start, beating Zarina Diyas and Saisai Zheng 6-2, 6-2. Simone Bolelli and Fabio Fognini, the No.5 seeds and Australian Open champions, were knocked out of the Gentlemen's Doubles Championship by Guillermo Garcia-Lopez and Malek Jaziri, who were joining forces for the first time in a Grand Slam tournament.

The hottest day of the year saw record usage of water taps, and a small electrical fire at the end of the day

The day began and ended with emergency services called into action. In the morning a large tree fell on to a passing car in Church Road, though nobody was hurt. In the evening, about an hour after play had finished, the London Fire Brigade was called to the All England Club after a small fire broke out in an electrical plant room located to the side of the Wingfield Restaurant. The Centre Court building was evacuated but the fire, which had been a result of the hot weather, was soon extinguished.

Feeling The Heat!

● **An historic day like this,** the hottest on record at The Championships, frankly deserved its own theme tune and it received one thanks to the sweltering hordes on The Hill, who decided there could only be one suitable anthem for such an afternoon. Cue a mass choir breaking into a chorus of Buster Poindexter's infectious: "Hot, hot, hot!"

● **Wimbledon's ball boys and girls** usually operate in hour-long spells but their shifts were reduced to 45 minutes because of the extreme heat. They were also issued with caps with special flaps for extra protection against the rays, incredibly useful even if they did make them look a little like a cross between spindly foreign legionnaires and loveable Labradors.

● **As the temperatures rose** on court, the serving speeds soared too. Milos Raonic sent down a 145mph rocket against Tommy Haas. Only two men had ever served a quicker one at Wimbledon.

It all left the 37-year-old Haas, who has probably suffered more injuries than in an entire series of *ER*, enjoying a little daydream about what it would be like to be able to serve like the Canadian.

"You know, that serve is... you know, I wish I had a serve like that just one time in a match just to see how that would feel," smiled the German veteran, almost lost in wonder.

"I was joking with my surgeon after the last surgery on my shoulder that maybe we could put some titanium in there where I could maybe just get more speed... but it wasn't possible."

Milos Raonic produced the third fastest serve in The Championships' history

● **Thanks to the weather forecasters,** Wimbledon had never been better prepared for the heatwave and had contingency plans in place to ensure that the crowds could get their water bottles regularly filled up around the grounds.

● **St John Ambulance,** which deals with emergencies at Wimbledon, reported that, remarkably, only two people needed to be taken to hospital on this day to be treated for heat-related ailments and both were soon released.

DAY FOUR
THURSDAY 2 JULY

Has anyone ever had a career of such contrasting fortunes at The Championships as Rafael Nadal? In his five appearances between 2006 and 2011 the Spaniard reached the final of the Gentlemen's Singles Championship each time and won the title twice. In his next three appearances, however, he lost in the second round to Lukas Rosol (world No.100), in the first round to Steve Darcis (world No.135) and in the fourth round to Nick Kyrgios (world No.144). Given the difficult year Nadal had endured since the summer of 2014, even the most ardent of his supporters might have feared the worst when he faced the flamboyant German, Dustin Brown, in the second round. Brown was ranked No.102 in the world, but, just as Rosol, Darcis and Kyrgios had done before him, played one of the matches of his life to beat Nadal 7-5, 3-6, 6-4, 6-4.

Dustin Brown produced the win of his career to upset Rafael Nadal in the second round. Nadal (right) fought back and was on the verge of sending the match into a fifth set

The Centre Court earthquake bore many similarities to Nadal's defeat by Rosol. Once again Nadal faced a big-hitting giant (Brown is 6ft 5in tall) who bombarded him with huge serves, went for broke on his ground strokes and denied the former world No.1 time to settle. Nevertheless, Brown also hit some beautifully judged drop shots and volleys. "On this court especially, you meet players that don't want to play from the baseline sometimes," Nadal said afterwards. "You cannot have mistakes against a player like him with that big serve. He had nothing to lose. He was serving first and second almost the same speed. I didn't have any rhythm at all. I didn't hit three balls in a row the same way."

"Dreddy" – so-called because of his dreadlocked hair, which has not been cut for 11 years – has a tattoo of his Jamaican father on the left side of his abdomen, which he patted at various stages of the match. He said his game plan had been to take Nadal out of his comfort zone. "If I would stay in the back and rally with him left, right, that would not be a very good match for me, I know that," Brown said. "Obviously I try to play my game. Even if I miss a few returns or whatever, it's also good if he doesn't get that many hits and obviously doesn't get into a rhythm."

Brown, who has a German mother, has been a journeyman professional for most of his career, sometimes barely making enough money to make ends meet. At one stage he drove from tournament to tournament in a camper van which doubled up as his overnight accommodation. At other times he has strung rivals' rackets in order to help pay his bills. He has never been ranked above No.78 in the world and has never reached a singles final on the main tour.

Brown was most effective in taking the net away from Nadal

As far as Nadal was concerned, however, it was an accident waiting to happen. The Spaniard has not quite been the same since he won his ninth French Open title the previous summer. A wrist injury and appendicitis kept him off the court for much of the second half of 2014 and not even his favourite period of the year, the European clay court season, could revive his fortunes in 2015, although his form picked up a little. He suffered only his second defeat in 71 matches at the French Open when he was beaten in the quarter-finals by Novak Djokovic, who had lost all six of their previous meetings at Roland Garros. Although Nadal went into The Championships having won his first grass court title for five years in Stuttgart, he was still clearly vulnerable, especially against an opponent who had beaten him on grass in Halle the previous year.

Nadal, who said he did not know whether he would ever be able to rescale the heights he had previously climbed at Wimbledon, was typically philosophical in defeat. "At the end of the day, that's sport," he said. "Obviously today is a bad moment for me. I just need to accept that these kind of things can happen. I have done that all my career. I'll keep going. It's not the end. It's a sad moment for me, but life continues." When he was asked by a journalist whether he would be staying in London for a while, Nadal showed he had not lost his sense of humour. "I don't have more work here in London, so if you want to use the house, it's going to be free tomorrow," he said.

(Left) It was the fourth time in four years at Wimbledon that Nadal had been knocked out by a player outside the top 100

WIMBLEDON IN NUMBERS

9

Per cent of return games won by Nadal during his last four Wimbledon losses, compared to his career average of 33

While Nadal was left to plan fishing expeditions and trips to the golf course back in Majorca, two of his fellow members of the so-called "Big Four" progressed with few alarms. Roger Federer beat Sam Querrey 6-4, 6-2, 6-2, while Andy Murray beat Robin Haase 6-1, 6-1, 6-4.

Querrey offered some stern resistance in the first set, but Federer eased to victory in just 81 minutes. Murray needed only six more minutes than that to beat Haase, who has given him trouble in the past. "In Grand Slams you have to try to conserve energy when you can because the two weeks can be quite draining physically and mentally," Murray said. Having not been at his best in the first round against Mikhail Kukushkin, Murray was pleased with his second-round performance. "The first couple of sets were excellent," he said. "Even in the third set some of the points were very good. I moved well today and hit the ball a lot cleaner from the back of the court. It was a good match." The win sent Murray into a third-round meeting with Italy's Andreas Seppi, who recovered well to beat 18-year-old Borna Coric, one of the game's most exciting prospects, 4-6, 6-4, 6-7(3), 6-1, 6-1.

The last time Britain had two men through to the last 32 was in 2002, but Murray found himself joined in the third round by a fellow countryman for the first time when James Ward beat the Czech Republic's Jiri Vesely 6-2, 7-6(4), 3-6, 6-3. However, Aljaz Bedene's hopes of strengthening the British contingent were dashed when he was beaten 4-6, 6-3, 2-6, 4-6 by Viktor Troicki.

Ward, who got into the main draw with a wild card, quickly took charge after the start of his match on No.2 Court was briefly delayed by the first rain of The Championships. The big-serving Vesely was ranked 64 places above Ward at No.45 in the world, but the Briton soon stamped his authority on the match. Ward, whose victory ensured that he would climb into the world's top 100 for the first

(Opposite page) Magdalena Rybarikova (top left) beat Ekaterina Makarova (top right) in the biggest upset of the day, while defending champion Petra Kvitova (bottom right), Sabine Lisicki (centre right) and Caroline Wozniacki (bottom left) all sailed through

Gael Monfils competed with his usual athletic and balletic flair

*Aljaz Bedene
narrowly missed
out on a place in
the third round*

time, held his nerve after Vesely took the third set. Ward and Murray have become good friends, with the Scot inviting the Londoner to join him at his training camps in Miami and Dubai. "He's always there supporting, always watching matches," Ward said. "Good habits rub off on you if you spend enough time around someone. He's been a big help to me and I'm grateful for that."

Ivo Karlovic beat the dying light and Alexandr Dolgopolov, winning 5-7, 6-3, 6-4, 6-7(4), 13-11 in a late finish on Court 18. Nikoloz Basilashvili, a 23-year-old Georgian making his debut at The Championships, claimed the notable scalp of Feliciano Lopez, beating the Spaniard 7-5, 3-6, 6-3, 2-6, 6-4.

Petra Kvitova, who dropped only one game against Kiki Bertens in the first round, maintained her impressive progress, crushing Kurumi Nara 6-2, 6-0 in 58 minutes, though she insisted that the scoreline was misleading. "It really wasn't easy," the defending champion said. "We played a few games that were really close. I'm just glad that I won. I still have a lot of space where I can improve for the next match. That's a good sign."

Ekaterina Makarova, the No.8 seed, was the biggest casualty in the Ladies' Singles Championship when she was beaten 2-6, 5-7 by Magdalena Rybarikova. Alize Cornet, who had knocked out Serena Williams 12 months earlier, fell to Olga Govortsova, who won 7-6(6), 2-6, 6-1. Kristyna Pliskova, enjoying a rare moment in the spotlight following her sister Karolina's exit, beat Svetlana Kuznetsova, the No.26 seed, 3-6, 6-3, 6-4, while Casey Dellacqua beat Elina Svitolina, the No.17 seed, 7-6(3), 6-3. Sabine Lisicki, the 2013 runner-up, recovered well to beat Christina McHale 2-6, 7-5, 6-1.

Lleyton Hewitt joined forces with Thanasi Kokkinakis to reach the second round of the doubles with a typically spirited comeback. The Australians beat Marin Draganja and Henri Kontinen 6-7(6), 3-6, 7-6(1), 6-2, 8-6 after almost four hours on court. Bob and Mike Bryan, playing their first match since the French Open after Mike suffered a torn stomach muscle, got their 17th consecutive campaign at The Championships off to an impressive start, beating Gero Kretschmer and Alexander Satschko 6-3, 6-4, 6-3.

*Lleyton Hewitt
kept his last
Championships
alive with a win in
doubles alongside
Thanasi Kokkinakis
on the newly re-laid
Court 14, back in
play after a year's
absence*

A Gift From Andy

• **The Duchess of Cornwall** ended up with a most unusual, if hardly the most fragrant, souvenir on her visit to Wimbledon – the world's most expensive wristband.

After Andy Murray's splendid performance against Robin Haase on No.1 Court, the Scot hurled his wristband towards the crowd, it landing in the hands of Philip Brook, the Chairman of the All England Club, who then passed it on to the Duchess.

When the pair met later, the former champion revealed: "The Duchess opened up her bag and my wristband was in there." The gift, he had to admit with a rueful smile, was "very sweaty".

But the Duchess made good use of her prize. Having got Murray to sign the band, she put it up for auction on eBay to raise money for the charity of the player's choice, the Royal Veterinary College Animal Care Trust. It sold for £2,100.

• **Even when not playing,** how could you keep the mischievous Nick Kyrgios out of the limelight?

Determined to get a glimpse of his compatriots, Lleyton Hewitt and Thanasi Kokkinakis in a doubles match on a packed Court 14, Kyrgios, complete with those giveaway pink headphones, clambered onto a railing to peep over the hoardings, only to be ticked off and ordered by a steward to get down.

Once the official was out of view, though, the crowd started chuckling when the cheeky Australian briefly tried to climb back up.

James Ward would be wearing his strawberry-infused Ted Baker outfit into the third round

• **James Ward's breakthrough** progression to the third round with victory over Jiri Vesely brought a particular smile to the Briton's backers. Ward's kits, some of which have strawberries in their pattern, are designed by the international fashion firm Ted Baker, leaving company founder, designer and Ward's unlikely practice partner Ray Kelvin, a former Middlesex junior, to declare: "It's amazing what happens when you dress well. When you dress well you feel good."

• **How good is Roger Federer?** Some days he's just so brilliant that even his opponents feel like saluting. Like Sam Querrey, who was on the receiving end of the shot of The Championships – a 'hot dog lob'.

Trying to react to a Querrey volley, Federer seemed to get into a tangle with his feet positioning so ended up having to concoct a shot from between his legs, somehow executing an inch-perfect lob which forced the American to scurry back and try in vain to retrieve it.

"He hits shots that other guys don't hit," mused Querrey. "You know, you want to go over and give him a high five sometimes – but you can't do that!"

Federer laughed: "If you don't win the point, you do look a little bit silly!" But if you pull it off, you look like the genius he is.

NEW BALLS PLEASE!

Three of the 54,250 tennis balls used every year at The Championships are prepared for a nine-game hammering

It all begins in the Philippines, before taking in a journey of some 6,600 miles and briefly becoming the focus of the world's attention at SW19's iconic sporting venue. And yet, ultimately, you may well end up whacking it around for fun in your back garden. This, then, is the remarkable adventure of just one of the 54,250 tennis balls used at The Championships each year.

Each ball is created in the Slazenger factory in Bataan from materials which themselves have been imported from all over the world – clay from the US, silica from Greece, magnesium carbonate from Japan, zinc oxide from Thailand, sulphur from South Korea, rubber from Malaysia, petroleum naphthalene from China, glue from the Philippines and wool from New Zealand.

Tested in detail for bounce, weight and compression to conform with strict International Tennis Federation rules, each ball is imported into Britain from the Philippines in a sealed tube of three and brought to the All England Club amid a box of 72 balls.

Stored in an office adjacent to Centre Court, the tubes are kept at their ideal temperature of 68 degrees Fahrenheit, and on the morning of play they are delivered by trolley to the Championship Balls front office. There, the captains of the ball boy and girl teams pick up a drum of 22 or 24 ball tubes to take to the courts they are working on.

Only six balls are ever in play at the same time and they're changed after the first seven games and then after every nine games.

After it's taken a short and savage beating from players hammering it down the court at anything up to 145mph, the ball's short Wimbledon life may be over but its next adventure is just beginning…

OLD BALLS PLEASE!

After the ball has been placed back in its tin and put in a green bag beneath the umpire's chair, it is ready the following day for a new lease of life.

At the Used Balls kiosk adjacent to Court 14, tins of three are resold for £3 or six for £5, with a total of £15,000 from the proceeds going towards the schools' programme organised by the Tennis Foundation, Britain's biggest tennis charity, designed to get schoolchildren involved in the sport.

Meanwhile, buyers can wonder idly if their purchase might have been whacked by Roger or Rafa, Maria, Serena or Andy. It's a Wimbledon daydreamer's ultimate souvenir.

DAY FIVE
FRIDAY 3 JULY

H eather Watson remembers buying a poster of Serena Williams when she visited The Championships as a child. She also recalls the days when Williams used to visit the IMG Academy in Florida. "It was a big thing for her to come and train there," said Watson, who has been based at the academy since she was 12. "All of our teachers let us out of school to go and watch her play." A decade on and Watson found herself facing the very woman she had looked up to for so many years. If ever there was a third-round match guaranteed to be given

Centre Court billing this was it: Watson, the Briton with one of the warmest smiles in tennis, against Serena Williams, the world No. 1 and five-time champion.

(Above) Centre Court rose to cheer on Heather Watson in exuberant fashion, while Serena Williams (right) *was frustrated at seeing her early advantage squandered*

For all the pre-publicity, however, few would have expected the drama that was to follow on a deliciously warm summer's evening. Watson had never beaten a player ranked higher than No.8 in the world, while Williams was on a 23-match winning run at Grand Slam tournaments. In sport, nevertheless, you learn to expect the unexpected. Watson played better than she ever has and went within two points of victory until Williams, the ultimate competitor, recovered to win 6-2, 4-6, 7-5. It was arguable whether the Centre Court crowd had ever roared more loudly as Watson pushed the world's greatest player to the brink.

When Watson played Agnieszka Radwanska on the same court and at the same stage of The Championships three years earlier, she had made the mistake of going for broke from the start. This time the world No.59 knew there would be no reward in trying to outhit Williams, so instead she used her speed and athleticism to make her opponent hit as many balls as possible. Watson repeatedly kept the rallies going, retrieving balls from every corner of the court and surprising Williams with the quality of her ball-striking. The post-match statistics told their own story, with Watson making only 11 unforced errors to Williams' 33. When the chance came to attack, Watson did so with a combination of smoothly struck ground strokes, delicate drop shots and low-bouncing slices.

When Williams took the first set in just 25 minutes, however, it would have been hard to imagine what was to follow. From 2-2 in the second set Watson broke in four of Williams' next five service games and from 3-4 down she won six games in a row. When Watson served for the second set she double-faulted at 30-30, but after five more points the 23-year-old from Guernsey had levelled the match, to a massive roar from the crowd.

Williams had been turning up her own volume controls with huge screams of "Come on!" The tension was clearly getting to the American, who hit two successive double faults to go 3-0 down in the decider. Watson, incredibly, had two points for a 4-0 lead, but Williams won a marathon game to stay in contention. The drama intensified when Watson, leading 3-2, lost five points in a row from 40-0 up. Williams went 4-3 ahead, only for Watson to win the next two games. At 5-4 the Briton served for the match, recovered from 15-40 to deuce but was finally broken when she netted a backhand. Two games later Watson saved two match points with unreturned serves, but on the third Williams clinched victory with a thumping return.

Despite being two points from defeat, Williams resurrected her form to out-pace Watson in the end

"I was two points away from winning the match so I am pretty disappointed," Watson said after leaving the court to a standing ovation. "The atmosphere on the court was amazing and it really helped me and pushed me. I just wish I could have closed it out at the end." She added: "I've learned that I can compete with the best in the world and I can play really good tennis. I just need to use this to motivate myself for the future and know that I can be there, I can compete, and I can be at the top of the game." Williams, having set up a fourth-round meeting with her sister Venus, said that Watson should set her sights higher than reaching the world's top 20. "Heather played unbelievably," the American said. "She just did everything so well. I wasn't able to keep up."

Fans on The Hill (right) and even AELTC staff (above) were gripped by one of the matches of The Championships

It was a match that captivated not only the Centre Court crowd but also the millions watching on television. On Twitter, women players were mentioned more times than the men, with 71,000 and 59,000 mentions for Williams and Watson respectively, compared with 30,000 and 26,000 for Murray and Nadal. The cricketer Kevin Pietersen described Watson as "quite brilliant", while the singer Olly Murs tweeted: "What a warrior!"

With six players through to the third round of the Ladies' Singles Championship it was proving to be the best first week for the United States since 2005. Venus Williams beat Aleksandra Krunic 6-3, 6-2, while Coco Vandeweghe raced to a 6-2, 6-0 victory over Samantha Stosur, who described her own performance as "capitulation". However, Bethanie Mattek-Sands was beaten 7-5, 7-5 by Belinda Bencic in a match that featured 10 breaks of serve.

There was no doubting the focus of attention in the Gentlemen's Singles Championship as Nick Kyrgios came from a set down to beat Milos Raonic, the No.7 seed, 5-7, 7-5, 7-6(3), 6-3. This was one of the rare occasions when Raonic found himself out-served as Kyrgios hit 34 aces to the Canadian's 18. Kyrgios, who had lost to Raonic in the quarter-finals the previous year, double-faulted three times in the final game of the first set, but was never broken thereafter. Once again the No.26 seed attracted a large group of supporters, one of whom was wearing a Batman t-shirt. "I thought he was key in the match," Kyrgios said afterwards. "He was actually saying some really good things at crucial moments. I think he helped." Kyrgios also had his customary brushes with authority. He was given a code violation after throwing his racket so hard that it bounced into the crowd and was ordered to turn his Wimbledon headband inside out because the colours did not follow the White Clothing and Equipment Rule.

Grigor Dimitrov, who like Raonic had reached the semi-finals 12 months previously, also went out. The Bulgarian, who had been struggling to live up to the promise he had shown when he beat Andy Murray in the last eight here in 2014, was beaten 3-6, 4-6, 4-6 by Richard Gasquet. Meanwhile Novak Djokovic eased to a 6-3, 6-3, 6-3 victory over Bernard Tomic. The world No.1 took everything in his stride, including signing an artificial leg which a spectator had handed to him after the match.

WIMBLEDON IN NUMBERS

7 Heather Watson's age when Serena Williams claimed her first Grand Slam singles title in 1999

Denis Kudla recorded his second five-set victory of the week to beat Santiago Giraldo 6-2, 6-7(3), 2-6, 6-1, 6-3 and reach the fourth round of a Grand Slam tournament for the first time. The 22-year-old American had been given a wild card after reaching the final at Surbiton and winning the title at Ilkley in two grass court Challengers in the build-up to The Championships. His performances on grass were a striking example of the benefits of the new three-week gap between the end of the French Open and the start of The Championships.

A day that had begun with The Championships joining the national minute's silence for the victims of the Tunisia terrorist attack a week earlier – as a consequence play began 45 minutes later than usual at 12.15 – ended with John Isner and Marin Cilic locked in a marathon battle. After more than four and a quarter hours' play their third-round match was suspended because of fading light at 10-10 in the final set. Both men knew what it was like to be involved in such a contest: in 2010 Isner won the longest match in the history of The Championships when he beat Nicolas Mahut after more than 11 hours, while Cilic won the second longest match two years later by beating Sam Querrey after five and a half hours.

The top seeds in the gentlemen's and ladies' doubles both made smooth progress. Martina Hingis and Sania Mirza beat Kimiko Date-Krumm and Francesca Schiavone for the loss of only one game in just 45 minutes, while Bob and Mike Bryan beat Steve Johnson and Sam Querrey 6-1, 5-7, 7-6(3), 6-3 in an all-American contest. The Bryans were playing on No.3 Court but were well aware of what was happening on Centre Court between Serena Williams and Heather Watson. "We didn't watch it, we heard it," Mike said. "They showed the scoreboard up on Centre Court and people could see it from No.3 Court, and literally between points there would almost be a standing ovation."

(Far left) The All England Club observed the national one minute silence at midday, in memory of the victims of the Tunisia attacks

Last year's semi-finalists, Grigor Dimitrov (left) *and Milos Raonic* (below), *saw their Wimbledon campaigns ended unexpectedly early*

Heather's Hill

![Championships Day 5 Notebook badge]

- **Interviewed for Live @ Wimbledon,** Tim Henman was asked the burning question whether Aorangi Terrace, dubbed 'Henman Hill' in his honour, should now be rechristened 'Murray Mound' after a certain Scottish star.

  With mock indignation, he responded: "That's one of the worst questions I've ever been asked. It's Henman Hill forever! Actually, I'd have let it become Heather's Hill during the Heather Watson–Serena Williams match, but definitely not Murray Mound!"

  Yes, that's right. Andy has got his Wimbledon title. Surely, we can let Tim keep his hill?

- **Novak Djokovic** can usually never get off Centre Court without a short autograph session for his fans. Programmes, giant tennis balls, rackets, shirts... you name it.

  But after beating Bernard Tomic in the third round, even the champion was left astonished by one request from a wheelchair-bound fan.

  "This gentleman gave me his artificial leg and I wanted to be politically correct about it. I gave him my signature," smiled the ever-obliging Djokovic. "I hope it will make him feel better."

- **In an outbreak** of happy Anglo-Australian relations, the 'Fanatics' from Down Under started chanting, "If you love Heather Watson, clap your hands" during the Briton's epic match with Serena Williams. Much laughter ensued when Heather herself began clapping enthusiastically.

- **After Watson's agonising defeat,** Andy Murray led the plaudits to his fellow British No.1 on his Twitter page, writing: "Retweet if @HeatherWatson92 just made you feel really effing proud! Favourite if she made you feel really effing proud!" Watson was so chuffed that she revealed that she herself was one of the 37,000-plus who favourited the message.

- **Suzanne Strong, hairdresser** to the stars in the Wimbledon hair salon and nail bar, reported that she was as busy as ever at this edition, snipping away in the job she has loved for 30 years, even if she hadn't yet had any of the sort of unusual requests that players had made in previous years.

The Championships' hairdresser, Suzanne Strong

  "Players aren't usually very brave because they're quite superstitious and want to stick to the same hairstyle," said Suzanne, who's cut and styled many champions' thatches from Chrissie Evert to Rafael Nadal and that very nice man with very nice hair, Roger Federer.

  "But we did once have a Russian player who wanted one side coloured green and the other side purple to match the Wimbledon colours." Apparently, she didn't get too far – either at Wimbledon or in the fashion world.

  Not that Suzanne is one for gossip. Players value the salon as a discreet escape. Some, like Novak Djokovic, are chatty enough. "But some players don't want to talk, they just want a bit of peace and quiet and to chill out," said Suzanne. "And we respect that."

GOODNIGHT WIMBLEDON

Just a few hours earlier, these Grounds were all hustle and bustle, packed with 28,000 people, a theatre teeming with cheers, laughs and sighs. On a lovely night like this, though, the All England Club, covered up and silently bathed in both moonlight and its own illuminations, just seems a picture of beautiful serenity as it dozes and dreams of the next day's installment of hectic drama.

DAY SIX
SATURDAY 4 JULY

I f you had conducted a straw poll before the start of play on the first Saturday to ask who had been the most impressive performer so far in the Ladies' Singles Championship, the winner would almost certainly have been Petra Kvitova. Serena Williams, the world No. 1, had gone to the brink of defeat against Heather Watson the previous evening and while the likes of Maria Sharapova, Agnieszka Radwanska and Victoria Azarenka had yet to drop a set between them, nobody was striking the ball better than the champion of 2011 and 2014. In crushing Kiki Bertens and Kurumi Nara in her first two matches, Kvitova had lost just three games.

(Above) Defending champion Petra Kvitova had been in imperious form

Ah, the glorious unpredictability of sport. By the end of the day Kvitova had departed The Championships, having been beaten 6-3, 5-7, 4-6 by 30-year-old Jelena Jankovic, a former world No. 1 whose best days had long seemed behind her. Jankovic had slipped to No.30 in the world rankings, having won only one minor title in the previous five years, but turned the form guide on its head to record one of the most unexpected results of the first week.

In the context of Kvitova's season, however, the result was not a complete surprise. The 25-year-old Czech had started the year well enough by winning the title in Sydney, but she went out of the Australian Open in the third round to Madison Keys and took a two-month break in the spring, saying she felt "exhausted" and "empty". Despite winning a clay court title in Madrid she went on to lose to Timea Bacsinszky in the fourth round of the French Open and had pulled out of her only pre-Championships grass court tournament in Eastbourne because of a virus.

Kvitova led Jankovic by a set and 3-1, only for her game to crumble. The defending champion served only six aces in the match, an unexpected return for a player with such a huge serve and one ideally suited to grass. Kvitova's ground strokes, another key part of her arsenal, deteriorated rapidly. The final game was typical as Kvitova made a series of forehand errors before netting a backhand on match point.

"Not to be in the second week of my favourite tournament is really sad," Kvitova said afterwards. "I'm not really sure what happened out there. I was up in the second set. Suddenly I felt like she was coming back, playing a little bit aggressive. Suddenly from my side, I didn't have an answer for it. My serve didn't help me at all this time as well. I was really struggling with each shot which I played." Jankovic also found it hard to explain the result. "I have played so poorly the last couple of years," she said. "Playing on grass is so difficult for me. It does not come naturally." The Serb, who has never had a reputation as a big server, was told afterwards that her total of 28 aces for the first week was bettered only by Keys' 42. "Is that for real?" she asked in disbelief.

Jelena Jankovic, a former world No.1, put on an inspirational performance to turn the match around

With Kvitova gone, the bottom half of the draw suddenly looked wide open. Radwanska, who would have been expecting to play Kvitova next, recorded her third successive straight-sets victory, beating Australia's Casey Dellacqua 6-1, 6-4, while Garbine Muguruza, the world No.20, showed great resilience to beat Angelique Kerber, the world No.10, 7-6(12), 1-6, 6-2. Keys, whose big game makes her a particular threat on grass, beat Tatjana Maria 6-4, 6-4, and Bacsinszky, the French Open semi-finalist, won 6-3, 6-2 against Sabine Lisicki, who failed to reach the quarter-finals for the first time in her last six appearances at The Championships.

The first Saturday is an occasion when a host of stars from a wide range of sports are invited into the Royal Box. Martina Navratilova, Boris Becker and the Sri Lankan cricketer Kumar Sangakkara were among them, but for the most part this was a parade of British talent, from the cricketers Geoffrey Boycott and Andrew Strauss to the golfers Justin Rose and Luke Donald, from the rugby players Matt Dawson and Chris Robshaw to the footballers Gary Lineker and Graeme Le Saux, and from the boxer Nicola Adams to the runner Jo Pavey.

The guests also included servicemen and women who had suffered life-changing injuries but went on to win medals at last year's Invictus Games. It was the perfect opportunity for British tennis to show the rest of British sport what it could do as Andy Murray took on Andreas Seppi on Centre Court while James Ward faced Vasek Pospisil on No.1 Court.

Murray's 6-2, 6-2, 1-6, 6-1 victory over Seppi reignited the debate among those who believe that there are times when players use medical time-outs deliberately to upset the rhythm of their opponents. While nobody accused either

NAME THE LEGEND

Sports stars who graced the Royal Box on 'Sports Saturday' included former Ireland rugby star Brian O'Driscoll (right), England fast bowler Jimmy Anderson (above) and (below, clockwise from top left) cyclist Joanna Rowsell, golfer Luke Donald, long distance runner Jo Pavey who in 2014 became the oldest female European champion, England rugby captain Chris Robshaw, Fed Cup captain Judy Murray, Paralympian David Weir, swimming legend Mark Foster and former England football captain Gary Lineker.

A SPORTING CELEBRATION

In the heart of a great sporting summer, Wimbledon once again opened the Centre Court Royal Box to the best of British sport, in what has become a welcome tradition on its Middle Saturday.

At the start of a week in which England's cricketers were to begin trying to regain the Ashes from Australia, Andrew Strauss, the former captain and now Director of Cricket, was alongside his record-breaking wicket-taker Jimmy Anderson, plus two of Test cricket's all-time great batsmen, England's Geoff Boycott and Sri Lankan Kumar Sangakkara.

There was also an invitation for the leaders of English rugby's bid to win the World Cup later in the year, with head coach Stuart Lancaster and captain Chris Robshaw joined by former England skippers Bill Beaumont and Matt Dawson.

Other luminaries included two Olympic champions, boxer Nicola Adams and cyclist Jo Rowsell, and Paralympic gold medallists, six-times wheelchair athletics champion David Weir and cyclists Neil Fachie and Craig Maclean.

Ryder Cup heroes Justin Rose and Luke Donald, the oldest-ever European 10,000m champion Jo Pavey, England footballing great Gary Lineker – "No diving in the box, Gary!" MC Sue Barker warned the old striker – and two Chairman's Special Guests, Martina Navratilova and Boris Becker, also had a great day.

Irish rugby legend Brian O'Driscoll even managed to enjoy a tennis lesson from Tim Henman before he joined the likes of current world squash champion Nick Matthew and former swimming world champion Mark Foster on Centre.

Yet while all these stars gained warm rounds of applause and cheers, it was as nothing compared to the reception offered to nine athletes who captured the nation's imagination in 2014 when they competed in the inaugural Invictus Games for wounded, injured and sick Armed Services personnel at London's Olympic Park.

The most rousing Centre Court ovation was reserved for those who had competed in the inaugural Invictus Games

102 mph

ROLEX 2.0

SETS GAMES POI

James WARD 2 1

v

Vasek POSPISIL • 1 3

CHALLENGES REMAINING

J. WARD 2

W. POSPISIL 2

wimbledon.com

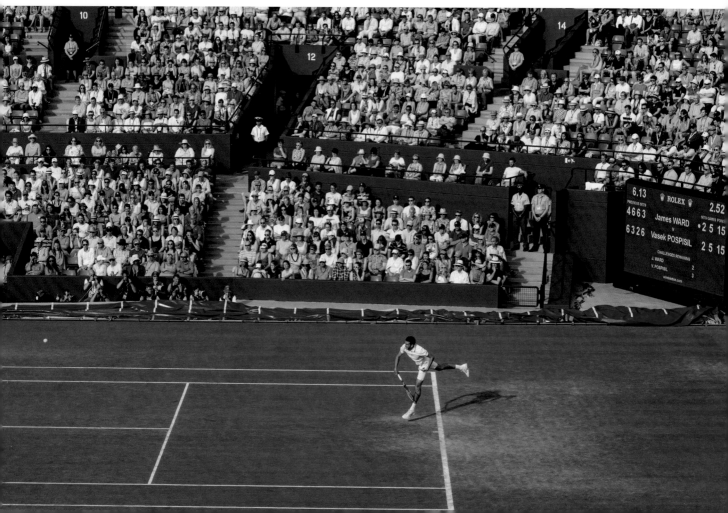

6.13 2.52

PREVIOUS SETS ROLEX SETS GAMES POINT

4 6 6 3 James WARD 2 5 15

v

6 3 2 6 Vasek POSPISIL 2 5 15

CHALLENGES REMAINING

J. WARD 2

V. POSPISIL 3

wimbledon.com

WIMBLEDON IN NUMBERS

4857

Metres covered by Gilles
Simon during his five-set
win over Gael Monfils,
who covered 4571.9m

Murray or Seppi of gamesmanship, there was no doubt that two time-outs helped to turn the course of the match. Murray was comfortably in control when Seppi sent for the trainer early in the third set for treatment on what he later said was a tight leg muscle. On the resumption the Italian won five games in a row, after which Murray took a time-out for treatment on his right shoulder. The Scot said that his shoulder had been tightening up towards the end of the second set and had got worse as he cooled down while Seppi was having treatment.

When play resumed it was Murray's turn to come out with all guns blazing as he won the next six games to claim victory. Seppi later denied that he had sent for the trainer as a tactical ploy but said he had joked with Murray at the end: "You used the same tactic as me when I called the physio."

Over on No.1 Court Ward and Pospisil fought for more than three hours for the prize of a first appearance in the second week of a Grand Slam event. The match was tight throughout. Ward, who had great support from the crowd, went up two sets to one before Pospisil recovered to win 6-4, 3-6, 2-6, 6-3, 8-6. The Canadian, who consulted a blue notebook during changeovers at critical stages of his matches throughout The Championships, served beautifully, especially in the deciding set. Ward said it had been "a chance missed" and thought the match had been decided by "a couple of points". He added: "If you can tell me there's a big difference between both of us, I'd love to know it."

Pospisil's reward would be a fourth-round meeting with Viktor Troicki, who beat Dustin Brown 6-4, 7-6(3), 4-6, 6-3. Brown was taught a lesson previously learned by Lukas Rosol, Steve Darcis and Nick Kyrgios: all four men failed to make further progress at The Championships after beating Rafael Nadal.

Roger Federer survived a serving bombardment from Sam Groth, a 6ft 4in Australian who holds the record for the fastest serve at a professional event (163mph). On this occasion Groth reached 147mph with one serve, which was just 1mph slower than Taylor Dent's record at The Championships, but lost 4-6, 4-6, 7-6(5), 2-6. Asked how he handled a match against such a big server, Federer said:

(Opposite page)
Andy Murray roared his way past Andreas Seppi **(top left)**, *while an inspired Vasek Pospisil* **(centre left)** *narrowly denied James Ward* **(bottom)**

Roger Federer **(bottom left)** *withstood a barrage of big serves from Sam Groth* **(below)**

Gael Monfils and Gilles Simon contested another five-set epic, finishing under the Centre Court roof

"The only thing I really have to change is my returning. The rest, the service games, I can control them myself. Once the return is played, then it's about reaction, especially when he's serve-volleying. You get to the next one, hit a pass. Really I think it's about keeping a short backswing on the return, trying to see it, and then also sometimes guessing the right way at the right times, remembering patterns where he's gone to, where he's been successful, and where not."

Ivo Karlovic did not break Jo-Wilfried Tsonga's serve once but still won 7-6(3), 4-6, 7-6(2), 7-6(9), though another of the game's big servers went out as Marin Cilic completed a 7-6(4), 6-7(6), 6-4, 6-7(4), 12-10 victory over John Isner. The match had been suspended because of bad light the previous evening at 10-10 in the deciding set. It lasted only two more games as Isner double-faulted on two of the last three points, having hit just one in the previous four and a half hours of the match. "It sucks," the American said afterwards in a succinct summary of his feelings.

Ground pass holders who stayed late were given an unexpected treat when they were allowed into Centre Court to watch the end of Gilles Simon's 3-6, 6-3, 7-6(6), 2-6, 6-2 victory over fellow Frenchman Gael Monfils. The match had begun on No.1 Court but was halted because of bad light just after 9pm. The players moved over to Centre Court, where the match finished under lights and a closed roof at 10.28pm.

Wimbledon had been hit by a torrential storm in the early hours of Saturday morning

The Wizard of Wimbledon

• **As the boys' singles** kicked off and the search to find a British champion continued, nobody was keener for the quest to be concluded than the last Briton to win, a man with one of the most revered names in sport.

Making a rare visit to the All England Club from his US home, Stanley Matthews Jnr, son and namesake of the late, great footballing knight, recalled when he won the title in 1962 against Alex Metreveli, later to become a gentlemen's singles finalist at Wimbledon.

Stanley, who found extra pressure from living in the shadow of the 'Wizard of the Dribble', never got beyond the second round at Wimbledon in his senior career but his legacy attracts media attention whenever a British boy makes the junior singles' final.

"Every time a Brit gets close to winning the boys' title the British press phone me up and say, 'How would you feel about somebody taking your record?' and my reply is always, 'I'd really like it so then you guys wouldn't phone me up any more!'" he joked.

• **He may have bowed out** against Viktor Troicki but Dustin Brown did not depart without one last glorious example of his maverick talent, playing an exquisite backhand drop shot return in the heat of battle which plopped over the net and span back over to his side of the court. "Everyone smiled, which is a good thing," grinned Brown. It was a trick shot that the great tennis entertainer Mansour Bahrami would have been proud of.

• **Despite hammering down** the second fastest serve in Wimbledon history at 147mph, Sam Groth inevitably still found Roger Federer too good. Nevertheless, the gentlemanly Australian still won

the title of best-mannered player, according to his compatriot Pat Cash who was impressed at the courtesy shown by the bearded athlete towards the ball boys and girls, as he made a point of thanking them each time they waited on him.

"Who is Clay the physio?", the world asked as Clay Sniteman treated Andy Murray

• **ATP physio Clay Sniteman** worked wonders on healing Andy Murray and Andreas Seppi on Centre Court, ensuring the name of the man who runs a physical therapy practice in Utah became the most googled non-player on Centre Court.

Roger Federer has called him a "Miracle Man", though the modest Sniteman once said that at his Weber State University offices "treating an elderly patient with a knee problem who wants to be able to play with his grandkids is every bit as important to me as a professional athlete."

THE CHAMPIONSHIPS AFTER DARK

A stunning view of the All England Club Grounds, Wimbledon Park and the bright lights of London, captured by a robotic camera positioned on the television crane during the late night Centre Court epic between Monfils and Simon.

DAY SEVEN
MONDAY 6 JULY

The growing feeling that the weather gods were smiling on The Championships was reinforced on Middle Sunday. After a week of beautiful weather with barely a drop of rain, the heavens finally opened over the All England Club on the morning of the traditional rest day. There is always an almost eerie peace about the place on Middle Sunday and for the first part of the day at least there was not even the usual trickle of players from the locker rooms to the practice courts. It was as if all the players were steeling themselves for "Manic Monday", which many observers regard as the most exciting day of The Championships. With the exception of the very last day, it is the only time when everyone left in singles competition gets to play on the same day.

Kevin Anderson (above) stretched both himself and Novak Djokovic by taking the first two sets

All 16 fourth-round singles matches were scheduled for a day of high-quality tennis. The only match that was not completed was a thrilling encounter between Novak Djokovic, the defending champion, and Kevin Anderson, the No. 14 seed. Anderson had demonstrated his grass court credentials by reaching the final at The Queen's Club the previous month and for two sets the South African's big serves and aggressive ground strokes kept Djokovic on the back foot. Anderson won two tie-breaks before Djokovic took the next two sets 6-1, 6-4. With the light fading fast the match was called off for the day at two sets apiece.

If there was one player you could never take your eyes off during The Championships it was surely Nick Kyrgios. Whenever the 20-year-old Australian set foot on court the excitement levels rose. Whether he was thumping huge winners or playing outrageous drop shots, arguing with officials or playing to the crowd, the world No.29 always had box-office appeal. His departure was totally fitting. In the course of a 5-7, 1-6, 7-6(7), 6-7(6) fourth-round defeat by Richard Gasquet, Kyrgios was briefly booed by the crowd for what they perceived as a lack of effort, was given a code violation for an audible obscenity, argued with the umpire over a change of kit and hugged a ball boy.

For Gasquet this was a chance to erase the painful memory of last year, when he lost to Kyrgios in the second round after failing to convert nine match points. This time the Frenchman played beautifully, hitting his majestic one-handed backhand with great power and precision to reach the quarter-finals for only the second time. Gasquet felt the pressure too, however, and demolished his racket after relinquishing two match points in the third set.

The most controversial moments of the match came after Kyrgios had been broken in the second game of the second set and had been penalised for swearing. Gasquet appeared to meet little resistance in winning his next service game, though Kyrgios emphatically denied any lack of effort. "Of course I tried," he later told a questioner at his post-match press conference. "Do you want to try to return Richard Gasquet's serve? I'll give you the racket and we'll see how many times you can return his serve." He added: "There were a lot of ups and downs. Obviously it was a tough, tough time, especially when he's not missing any balls. I'm getting frustrated myself. I feel as if I'm playing not how I should be playing. I'm angry at myself. Obviously I wasn't really happy with the way I was performing out there. I obviously lacked a bit of energy. I thought I responded well, though, to even come back and win the third set."

Kyrgios also hugged a ball boy – "I just felt like a hug, I guess," the Australian said afterwards – and had a tetchy exchange at a changeover with the umpire, James Keothavong, as he removed one of the two pairs of socks he had been wearing. "If you're going to get angry with me for that, that's another level,"

But Djokovic fought back to take the fourth before the light faded

The eventful match between Nick Kyrgios and Richard Gasquet included the young Australian getting into an argument with the umpire over the length of time it was taking for him to remove a pair of socks

WIMBLEDON IN NUMBERS

34

Combined appearances by Venus (18) and Serena Williams (16) in the main draw at The Championships

Kyrgios told him. "Mate, Rafa [Nadal] and stuff play 30 seconds in between points every time and all I'm doing is putting my sock back on."

The biggest surprise of the day in the gentlemen's singles was Gilles Simon's 6-3, 6-3, 6-2 victory over Tomas Berdych, which earned the Frenchman a place in the last eight of a Grand Slam tournament for only the second time. His next opponent would be Roger Federer, who reached his 45th Grand Slam quarter-final by beating Roberto Bautista Agut 6-2, 6-2, 6-3. The Spaniard became the eighth player in succession to fail to break Federer's serve. Asked how he had been able to hold serve 106 times in a row, Federer quipped: "Guys are returning terrible!"

Stan Wawrinka beat David Goffin in three tight sets, Marin Cilic ended Denis Kudla's run in four sets and Vasek Pospisil played two five-set matches in the course of the day. Having fought back to beat Viktor Troicki 4-6, 6-7(4), 6-4, 6-3, 6-3 in singles, Pospisil then joined forces with Jack Sock in the continued defence of their doubles title. Another back-from-the-brink comeback seemed to be on the cards until Jamie Murray and John Peers recovered to complete a 6-3, 7-6(6), 6-7(5), 3-6, 8-6 victory.

The latter result would have given particular pleasure to Murray's brother, Andy, who secured a quarter-final meeting with Pospisil by beating 36-year-old Ivo Karlovic 7-6(7), 6-4, 5-7, 6-4. Karlovic, the oldest man to reach the fourth round for 39 years, took his tally of aces in the tournament to 165, but Murray gave a tactical master class. Karlovic charged forward but Murray repeatedly passed or lobbed him, which was no mean feat against a 6ft 11in opponent. Karlovic said he could never remember having been lobbed as many times. Murray, reaching the quarter-finals for the eighth year in a row, also slowed down his first serve, giving Karlovic fewer opportunities to attack his second serve.

The most eagerly awaited match of the day had been the 26th meeting of Serena and Venus Williams and their sixth at the All England Club. The sisters had each won the title five times, but for some years now Serena had been the dominant force. Like a number of their previous meetings, however, the match proved an anti-climax as Serena eased to a 6-4, 6-3 victory. Both women appeared

(Opposite page) Richard Gasquet (top left), Gilles Simon (top right), Stan Wawrinka (bottom) and Vasek Pospisil (centre right) all advanced to the last eight, some more easily than others

Serena and Venus Williams contested their 26th match against each other, their sixth at Wimbledon

unwilling to challenge any contentious line calls and there was none of the usual fist-pumping from Serena. The sisters rarely enjoy playing each other and even their mother, Oracene, chose not to attend their latest meeting. Explaining her own downbeat demeanour, Serena said afterwards: "It's hard to feel excited about beating someone you root for all the time no matter what and you love so much and is your best friend in the world."

Two more Americans booked their places in the quarter-finals, giving the United States their best representation in the last eight since 2004. Madison Keys beat Olga Govortsova 3-6, 6-4, 6-1, while Coco Vandeweghe knocked out a seed for the third round in succession when she beat Lucie Safarova, the French Open runner-up, 7-6(1), 7-6(4), despite what she described as her worst performance of the Fortnight so far. Garbine Muguruza reached the quarter-finals for the first time when she beat the No.5 seed, Caroline Wozniacki, 6-4, 6-4, as did Timea Bacsinszky, who beat Monica Niculescu 1-6, 7-5, 6-2. Jelena Jankovic, the conqueror of Petra Kvitova, went down 5-7, 4-6 to Agnieszka Radwanska, Maria Sharapova beat Zarina Diyas 6-4,

Belinda Bencic's fine tournament ended at the hands of Victoria Azarenka, but fellow rising star Madison Keys (below) battled past Olga Govortsova in three

6-4 and Belinda Bencic's fine grass court season ended in a 2-6, 3-6 defeat to Victoria Azarenka.

Lleyton Hewitt's Wimbledon career finally came to an end when he was beaten in both the gentlemen's doubles and the mixed doubles. Hewitt and his fellow Australian, Thanasi Kokkinakis, went down 6-7(7), 3-6, 6-7(1) to the No.4 seeds, Jean-Julien Rojer and Horia Tecau, before Juan-Sebastian Cabal and Cara Black beat Hewitt and Casey Dellacqua 0-6, 6-3, 6-3. As the former world No.1 walked off for the last time a big Australian contingent on Court 18 sang, "There's only one Lleyton Hewitt". Jonathan Marray and Frederik Nielsen, the men's doubles champions in 2012, were beaten 1-6, 4-6, 6-7(6) by the No.2 seeds, Ivan Dodig and Marcelo Melo.

Three of the top four seeds went out on a day of surprises in the girls' singles. Anna Brogan, a 17-year-old Scot, took full advantage of her wild card to beat the No.1 seed, Marketa Vondrousova, 6-1, 6-2. Brogan had not won a match in her two previous appearances in the Junior Championships. Another Briton, Maia Lumsden, beat the No.3 seed, Dalma Galfi, 7-5, 6-3, while the No.4 seed, Anna Kalinskaya, was beaten 6-7(4), 4-6 by Viktoria Kuzmova.

Go Bro!

• **Andy Murray pumped** his fists excitedly in the middle of a very sober press conference following his defeat of Ivo Karlovic, before apologising to the media throng that he had just seen on the results screen in the interview room that his brother Jamie and John Peers had knocked holders Vasek Pospisil and Jack Sock out of the gentlemen's doubles.

This, Murray explained, was the usual way that he found out about his elder sibling's results because he rarely watched Jamie on TV and always had the feeling that whenever he did watch him live, he lost.

"When Jamie played the mixed doubles final here in 2007, I was just pacing around, away from Centre Court, checking the score from time to time," Murray said. "I only ran out for the last game when it looked like they might win."

• **One reporter,** who must have been affected by the heat or was perhaps just suffering a senior moment, had to beat a hasty retreat when, in Tomas Berdych's post-match press conference, he asked the No.6 seed, who had just been soundly thrashed by Gilles Simon: "Do you feel your form is good going into the quarter-finals?"

It left Berdych, already hardly in the best of moods, growling to the moderator, "Is he trying to make fun of me?" while the chastened questioner took one look at a seething 6ft 5in Czech and could only blurt out: "Sorry, sorry…"

• **A week after** his last singles match, this time it really was the final farewell for Lleyton Hewitt as he was knocked out of both the gentlemen's doubles and mixed doubles, and finished his last match to a rousing standing ovation on Court 18.

Nobody wanted him to go. As the 34-year-old, playing alongside compatriot Casey Dellacqua, was being defeated by Juan-Sebastian Cabal and Cara Black, the Australian 'Fanatics' in the crowd started chanting: "If you don't want Lleyton to retire, clap your hands."

There followed the longest, most heartfelt round of applause heard throughout the Fortnight.

• **All these years since** his flamboyant 1970s playing heyday, Ilie Nastase, Romania's two-time finalist and one of Wimbledon's greatest characters, remains hard to beat as a scene stealer. For while the Williams sisters were battling on Centre Court, the eye was constantly being drawn to the striking figure in the Royal Box clad in shiny full cream military regalia and sunglasses, looking for all the world as if he was plotting world domination.

The wonderful 68-year-old 'Nasty', who played for the Romanian Army's sports club Steaua, was proudly wearing his major general's uniform awarded to him by presidential decree.

Ilie Nastase came to the Royal Box dressed for the occasion

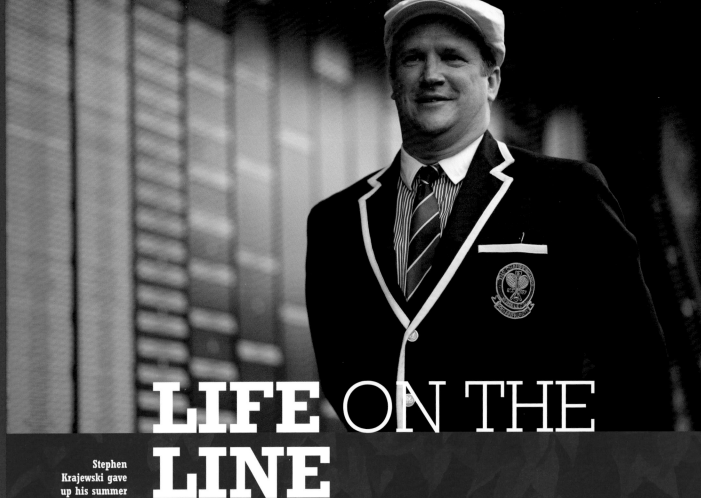

LIFE ON THE LINE

Stephen Krajewski gave up his summer holidays to work as a line judge during Wimbledon fortnight

More than 340 elegantly-attired umpires officiated at Wimbledon 2015 and for all of them, as marketing executive Stephen Krajewski discovered, it was a scorchingly wonderful, if sometimes challenging, experience.

For the London-based American, a decent club player who spends weekends umpiring at events around the country, it felt partly a reward and partly a rare ambition fulfilled when, like so many of the officials who'd gathered from all over the world from Australia to Kuwait, he used his work holiday to become part of the greatest show in tennis.

For starters, the 50-year-old had to look the part, getting kitted out from flat-capped head to immaculately-shod toe in blazered Ralph Lauren finery. "I've never been more expensively clad," laughed Stephen, whose mother, over from America, even came along to take snaps during the fitting process.

After meeting his new colleagues in the Buttery, from 35-year veterans to SW19 debutants like him, Stephen's baptism of fire was a gentlemen's doubles match on Court 19 featuring defending champions Jack Sock and Vasek Pospisil against Sergiy Stakhovsky and Sam Groth, the man with the fastest recorded serve in history at 163.4mph.

"I thought the speed, especially from Sam Groth's quickest serves, would be the biggest challenge but it was okay," said Stephen. "The hardest thing was keeping concentration, especially when it's so hot. The danger is you think about the heat rather than the line."

His most deflating moment was crying fault too early only to see a puff of chalk and have his mistake instantly overruled. "It makes your heart sink but I'd like to think it was my only glaring error in about 22 hours on court. So, hey, not bad…"

Stephen's bosses concurred. The range of marks for his performance, handed out by his chair umpires, were positive and he hopes to be back in 2016.

As for his marks for sartorial elegance, he knew he must have passed the test when, while having his picture taken next to the fountain, Greg Rusedski wandered by and commented: "Hey, looking good!" It made Stephen's fortnight complete.

DAY EIGHT
TUESDAY 7 JULY

The Ladies' Singles Championship had produced plenty of shocks in the first seven days, but come the quarter-finals only one unseeded player was left. Coco Vandeweghe, the world No.47, had already claimed the scalps of three seeded players in Karolina Pliskova, Samantha Stosur and Lucie Safarova. Could she take a fourth against Maria Sharapova, the No.4 seed? There could be no doubting Vandeweghe's sporting pedigree. Her grandfather played for the New York Knicks basketball team in the 1950s, her mother swam for the United States in the 1976 Olympics and her uncle was general manager of the Denver Nuggets basketball team. Coco's real name is Colleen, but her mother gave her four children nicknames which stuck: Coco, Beau, Honnie and Crash. Coco was named after her grandmother, a former Miss America.

Coco Vandeweghe brought every bit of her New York spirit to Centre Court in pushing Maria Sharapova (right) to produce her best tennis

A bright future had been predicted for Vandeweghe after she was crowned US Open junior champion in 2008, but for several years she struggled to make her mark at senior level, winning only two matches in her first 13 Grand Slam tournaments. The turning point came last year when she decided she needed to become more professional, hired a fitness trainer and improved her nutrition. There would be no more visits to In-N-Out Burger for her favourite order of a "double-double" with French fries and a milkshake. By the end of the year she had climbed 70 places to No.40 in the world rankings and demonstrated her liking for grass by winning the title at 's-Hertogenbosch.

The confidence Vandeweghe had derived from her progress to her first Grand Slam quarter-final was evident. Her game is built on power and Sharapova was soon feeling the weight of her booming serves and bold ground strokes. Vandeweghe never looked over-awed, as she showed when she complained to the umpire, Eva Asderaki-Moore, alleging that Sharapova had been distracting her by moving around as she hit her second serves. The umpire did not agree with Vandeweghe's complaint, but the American refused to let the subject drop. "I said if she had a problem speaking to Maria, if she was too scared to do it, I had no problem speaking to her," Vandeweghe said later.

Sharapova, standing firm, took the first set and served for the match at 5-4 in the second, only for Vandeweghe to break back. Encouraging the Centre Court crowd to turn up the volume, Vandeweghe took the set into a tie-break, which she won 7-3. Sharapova quickly regained control by going 3-0 up in the decider, but Vandeweghe, continuing to whip up the crowd, fought back to 3-2, only to lose the next three games and the match as Sharapova triumphed 6-3, 6-7(3), 6-2. "I enjoyed the crowd out there," Vandeweghe said afterwards. "I'm happy with my progress through the tournament and I'm happy with the whole experience of it."

(Top) Sharapova had seen the second set snatched from her, before fighting back

(Above) Vandeweghe later said she had enjoyed the occasion

The day at the All England Club had begun with The Championships joining in the nation's minute of silence to commemorate the 10th anniversary of the London bombings. It was quite a contrast with the scene on Centre Court later in the day as Serena Williams and Victoria Azarenka contested what was quite possibly the noisiest match of the Fortnight. The heavyweight showdown between two ferocious competitors was played to a backdrop of noise as both women threw themselves into their shots, greeting winners with huge roars of "Come on!" The player boxes were equally animated, with Azarenka's hitting partner, Sascha Bajin, a stalwart member of the Williams camp until earlier in the year, particularly pumped up.

At times some spectators laughed at the noise from both players. Azarenka was not amused. "It's so annoying because guys grunt," she said afterwards. "I was practising next to [Rafael] Nadal and he grunts louder than me – and nobody notices that. Why? I don't understand why. Both women on the court were trying their hardest and giving everything, and they make noises. Is that a problem for tennis? It happens in every sport."

With her aggressive returns of serve Azarenka gives Williams more problems than most and the match developed into a full-blooded thriller before the American won 3-6, 6-2, 6-3 to reach her ninth

(Far left) *Victoria Azarenka proved herself returned to full fitness*

Serena Williams admitted that playing Azarenka always brings out the best in her

The pair greeted each other warmly at the net after the match

(Opposite page) *Garbine Muguruza* **(top right)** *proved a delighted winner over Timea Bacsinszky* **(top left)**, *while Agnieszka Radwanska* **(bottom right)** *triumphed against Madison Keys* **(bottom left)**

Wimbledon semi-final. Azarenka, who had been rebuilding her world ranking after missing most of 2014 with a foot injury, won the first set after breaking serve in the fourth game. But the match turned in the middle of the second as Williams' greater power finally gave her the edge. The world No.1 hit 17 aces to Azarenka's seven and 46 winners to Azarenka's 20. The two players embraced at the end in a warm demonstration of mutual respect. "I feel like me and Victoria always have really wonderful matches," said Williams. "Whenever I see her name I get excited because I feel like there's going to be an opportunity to see how well I'm doing."

While the top half of the draw had featured a number of big-name confrontations – with another to follow as Williams and Sharapova prepared to meet in the semi-finals – the bottom half was witnessing the emergence of some new talent. Timea Bacsinszky had already proven her ability by reaching the semi-finals of the French Open, but her quarter-final opponent, Garbine Muguruza, had gone into the Fortnight having won only one match in her two previous appearances at The Championships. However, the world No.20 became the first Spanish woman to reach the semi-finals for 18 years when she won 7-5, 6-3 with a pleasing combination of powerful hitting and intelligent tactics. She was asked afterwards which players she had learned from. "I always like to take little parts of every player," she said. "You see the Williams sisters, the power, the aggression, the confidence they have in themselves. You see Maria [Sharapova]. She has a very good mentality and she's very focused during the whole match. Or [Martina] Hingis. She is very talented."

The one player in the bottom half of the draw with a wealth of experience at The Championships was Agnieszka Radwanska, who reached the semi-finals for the third time in four years by beating Madison Keys 7-6(3), 3-6, 6-3. It was a classic contrast of styles as Radwanska attempted to counter Keys' power with her variety and tactical nous. Keys hit 12 aces, taking her total for The Championships to 59.

Earlier, The Championships had observed the national minute's silence in memory of the London bombings

WIMBLEDON IN NUMBERS

18
Years since a Spanish woman had reached the singles semi-finals at Wimbledon, Arantxa Sanchez-Vicario in 1996

The first match on No.1 Court had seen Novak Djokovic complete his comeback from two sets down to beat Kevin Anderson 6-7(6), 6-7(6), 6-1, 6-4, 7-5. Djokovic, winning on the 30th anniversary of his coach Boris Becker's first triumph at The Championships at the age of 17, described the match as "one of the most difficult in my Wimbledon career". The fourth-round match resumed at the start of the fifth set, having been called off the previous evening because of fading light. Anderson had served superbly the previous day and was quickly back into a good rhythm. At times Djokovic looked ill at ease, but the defending champion took his chance when Anderson served two double faults at 5-5. Djokovic's tension had been evident when he startled a ball girl by screaming for his towel. "It was a very intense fifth set," Djokovic said afterwards. "I'm definitely going to try to apologise to her if I did something wrong."

Rohan Bopanna and Florin Mergea served up the biggest surprise in the Gentlemen's Doubles Championship when they beat Bob and Mike Bryan, the top seeds, 5-7, 6-4, 7-6(9), 7-6(5). The No.2 seeds also went out as Jonathan Erlich and Philipp Petzschner beat Ivan Dodig and Marcelo Melo 4-6, 6-2, 6-2, 6-4. Jamie Murray, the 2008 Mixed Doubles Champion alongside Jelena Jankovic, reached the semi-finals of the gentlemen's doubles for the first time when he partnered John Peers to a 6-4, 7-6(3), 6-3 victory over Alexander Peya and Bruno Soares. "We've beaten a lot of the top teams over the last couple of years," Murray said afterwards. "I think we've been going in the right direction over the last 18 months and to be honest I think we deserve to be where we are."

Britain's Katie Swan, the No.5 seed, was the highest seed still standing in the girls' singles after Russia's Olesya Pervushina beat China's Shilin Xu, the No.2 seed, 6-3, 4-6, 6-3. Swan, who beat Deria Nur Haliza 6-1, 6-2, was joined in the last 16 by another Briton, Anna Brogan, who beat Katarina Zavatska 6-1, 6-3. Duck Hee Lee, the No.2 seed in the boys' singles, had a day to remember. Having warmed up Djokovic in the morning, the Korean saved two match points before beating Marc Polmans 6-7(6), 7-6(3), 9-7.

Novak Djokovic survived an overnight delay to beat Kevin Anderson in five sets, despite a rain-delayed start

Starstruck By Zorro

• Garbine Muguruza sounded almost as excited about a chance meeting in the Wimbledon dining room as she did about beating Timea Bacsinszky to reach her first Grand Slam semi-final.

Having come across Antonio Banderas, who had appeared in SW19 the previous week to watch his old friend Rafa Nadal, the young Spaniard admitted she was so nervous that, at first, she could barely speak, but the lively 21-year-old soon ended up in deep conversation with the film star about his latest movie.

She could not confirm, however, whether the tennis fan was so impressed with her swashbuckling ground strokes that he was reminded of his Zorro heyday.

• The age-old grumbling about grunting resumed as Victoria Azarenka and Serena Williams turned up the volume with their splendid Centre Court encounter.

This time, sick to death of being questioned about the subject and demanding reporters looked at the "good stuff" in the women's game instead, Azarenka aimed a volley at one interrogator: "Stop bringing up this ridiculous stuff. Let's put aside the noise, how she looks and look at the game. The game proved itself today," said the Belarusian. "I'm tired of these questions. It's annoying as guys grunt."

• Andy Murray's inspiration to all young British players became clear on a day when teenager Katie Swan made impressive progress in the girls' event and then told of her excitement at being backed by the 2013 champion.

Katie Swan was excited to have social media support from Andy Murray

American-based Swan, the No.5 seed who was the Australian Open girls' singles runner-up in January, reached the last 16 and explained how she had been buoyed by Murray's good luck message on Twitter to her and another promising British player, Ali Collins, who also hails from the Scot's hometown of Dunblane.

"It was really nice of him," said Swan, one of Britain's best young prospects. "And it's been cool watching him practice. Amazing."

• A couple of days after USA's women had won the FIFA World Cup, you could see how the footballing festival had captured athletes' imaginations as Kristina 'Kiki' Mladenovic decided to show off some novel big match preparations to her Twitter followers.

One of the bright young hopes of French tennis was filmed doing an impressive spot of keepy-uppy – or as she put it "trying to improve my right foot juggle" – and then a fancy stepover trick outside the locker rooms as she and Daniel Nestor waited for their mixed doubles match.

DAY NINE
WEDNESDAY 8 JULY

O
f all the qualities shared by the so-called "Big Four" of men's tennis, you could argue that the greatest has been their consistency. From Roger Federer's record-breaking run of 63 consecutive appearances in Grand Slam tournaments to Rafael Nadal's sequence of nine French Open triumphs in 10 years, from Novak Djokovic's 25 appearances in a row in Grand Slam quarter-finals to Andy Murray's run of eight consecutive quarter-finals at The Championships, the record books are full of statistics underlining not only the brilliance of the four men but also their longevity.

Richard Gasquet produced one of the matches of the tournament with his win over Stan Wawrinka

The Frenchman is an expert at racket re-gripping, which he can do in 17 seconds

When the semi-final line-up took shape here it was no surprise that three of the four places were filled by men who have dominated the sport for the best part of a decade. Djokovic, Federer and Murray were joined in the semi-finals by Richard Gasquet, who seemed to surprise himself with his achievement. "When you see the line-up of Federer, Djokovic and Murray – and then me – well, I'm amazed," the Frenchman said.

Gasquet earned his place in the last four by beating Stan Wawrinka 6-4, 4-6, 3-6, 6-4, 11-9 in an epic quarter-final, while the three big guns all won in straight sets. Djokovic beat Marin Cilic, the US Open champion, 6-4, 6-4, 6-4, Federer finally dropped his serve but still coasted to a 6-3, 7-5, 6-2 victory over Gilles Simon, and Murray was too good for Vasek Pospisil, winning 6-4, 7-5, 6-4. If Wawrinka had won, it would have been the first time for 20 years that the top four seeds had reached the semi-finals at Wimbledon.

Vasek Pospisil tried to close the net to preserve his tired legs

For Murray it was a day to remind himself of how far he had come since his defeat to Grigor Dimitrov in the previous year's quarter-finals. That reverse had ended Murray's run of six successive semi-final appearances at The Championships, but it was a result in keeping with his year. Having returned at the start of the 2014 season following back surgery, Murray had struggled to look capable of rescaling his former heights. A parting of the ways with Ivan Lendl had left him searching for a new coach and he had arrived at the All England Club in 2014 having only just started working with Amelie Mauresmo. Winning three titles in the autumn helped to restore some confidence during a year in which he slipped out of the world's top 10 for the first time since 2008, but when his season ended with a crushing 0-6, 1-6 defeat at the hands of Federer at the Barclays ATP World Tour Finals it was clear that there was still a sizeable gap between Murray and the top players.

But Andy Murray had little trouble responding

Murray, nevertheless, had always said that he needed time to work with Mauresmo before she could be judged and after a winter training camp in Miami the Scot looked a very different player at the start of 2015. He reached his first Grand Slam final for 18 months at the Australian Open, played in his first Masters 1000 final for two years in Miami and claimed the first clay court titles of his career in Munich and Madrid before reaching the semi-finals of the French Open. Winning his fourth Queen's Club title in his only tournament in the build-up to The Championships proved that his grass court game was in good shape.

Pospisil looked in vain for inspiration from the famous blue notebook which he took on court with him. The 25-year-old Canadian never did reveal exactly what he had written inside it. Pospisil, who was appearing in his first Grand Slam singles quarter-final, had played 10 sets of tennis two days earlier and admitted afterwards that he had felt heavy-legged. Knowing there would be only one winner if he got drawn into too many long rallies, Pospisil charged forward in the hope of finishing off points quickly, but Murray repeatedly picked him off at the net.

After two breaks for rain, the roof was closed for the last set and a half. Pospisil was broken at 5-5 in the second set after being given a time violation at 30-30 by Pascal Maria, the umpire, when he took too long to serve; at Grand Slam events players are allowed to take only 20 seconds between points. Pospisil later called Maria's ruling "ridiculous" and claimed that top players were rarely given time violations. He was penalised again under the same rule when he dropped serve for the last time in the third set. The result meant that Andy and Jamie Murray were the first brothers to reach the semi-finals of the gentlemen's singles and gentlemen's doubles respectively at the same Championships since the Australians John and Neale Fraser did so in 1962.

Andy Murray's reward for his 10th win in a row on grass would be a semi-final against Federer, who maintained his smooth progress with victory over Simon. The only consolation for the Frenchman was that he ended Federer's run of 116 unbroken service games in succession, dating back to the first round of the previous month's tournament in Halle. Yet Federer expressed a modicum of relief that the streak had ended. "Now I can just focus on the normal things, not whether I'm going to hold serve or not," he said. Federer extended his own record for Grand Slam semi-final appearances by reaching his 37th, while his 10th appearance in the last four at the All England Club would leave him just one behind Jimmy Connors' record.

Djokovic reached his sixth successive semi-final at The Championships by recording his 13th victory in a row over Cilic. The world No.1 won with a single break in each set and was pleased to have got the job done quickly in his third successive day on court after his fourth-round match had been spread over two days. "I didn't know how my body was going to feel but I was hoping I would play well, which I have done," he said. After the match the world No.1 sought out the ball girl he had shouted at the previous day. "I've talked with the girl and she said she didn't mind," Djokovic said. "I apologised if it was anything that I did."

In the semi-finals Djokovic might have been expecting a repeat of his recent French Open final against Wawrinka, but the champion of Roland Garros lost to Gasquet in one of the matches of the tournament. Purists would have enjoyed the sight of two players with classic one-handed backhands as Gasquet, one of the game's great stylists, fought back from two sets to one down to complete a

(Opposite page)
Novak Djokovic was in imperious form despite playing for a third day in a row

Marin Cilic struggled to find any opening against the defending champion

LIFE UNDER COURT 15

They are such an important part of Wimbledon that it seemed only fitting that the 250 brilliant ball boys and girls on duty should now have their own new, dedicated complex beneath Court 15 to prepare and relax. Roger Federer, who opened the facility, told the youngsters: "You guys are some of the best in the world." And he should know, having been a nifty 12-year-old ball boy himself in Basle.

Martina Hingis rolled back the years alongside Sania Mirza, reaching the semi-finals of the ladies' doubles

Roger Federer shrugged off dropping serve for the first time all tournament against Gilles Simon

memorable victory. The world No.20's mental strength has been questioned in the past, but he stuck to his task despite failing to serve out the match at 5-3 in the fifth set. Thereafter Wawrinka held serve five times in a row to stay in the match before Gasquet finally made his breakthrough. "It was very difficult for me to lose that serve at 5-3," Gasquet said afterwards. "Then I kept fighting. That made the difference."

Martina Hingis and Sania Mirza, the No.1 seeds in the Ladies' Doubles Championship, secured their place in the semi-finals by beating Casey Dellacqua and Yaroslava Shvedova 7-5, 6-3. Hingis, who first won the same title here in 1996, said her run this year was "like a dream come true". She added: "Wimbledon is the most prestigious Grand Slam. You step on the grass court out here and it is pure joy. I'm really enjoying the adventure." Ekaterina Makarova and Elena Vesnina, the No.2 seeds, beat Cara Black and Lisa Raymond 6-3, 4-6, 8-6, while the No.3 seeds, Bethanie Mattek-Sands and Lucie Safarova, were beaten 3-6, 2-6 by Raquel Kops-Jones and Abigail Spears.

Mike Bryan and Mattek-Sands, who won the title together at the French Open, moved into the quarter-finals of the Mixed Doubles Championship by beating Michael Venus and Raluca Olaru 7-6(3), 7-5. Marcin Matkowski and Vesnina joined them in the last eight after beating Lukasz Kubot and Andrea Hlavackova 6-7(4), 6-4, 11-9 in a marathon that lasted more than two and a half hours.

WIMBLEDON IN NUMBERS

53 Years since two brothers reached the semi-finals of the gentlemen's singles and gentlemen's doubles at Wimbledon

Patrik Niklas-Salminen, competing in only his second grass court event, beat Duck Hee Lee, the No.2 seed, 6-4, 6-0 in a day of upsets in the boys' singles. Michael Mmoh, Marcelo Tomas Barrios Vera and Viktor Durasovic, seeded No.4, No.6 and No.8 respectively, also lost. Britain's Katie Swan was one of only two seeds to survive in the girls' singles. Swan beat Sofia Kenin 7-6(1), 6-2, while Anna Blinkova, the No.12 seed, beat Usue Maitane Arconada, the No.6 seed, 6-4, 6-3.

Feds In His Sights

- **On a great day for celebrity spotters** – everyone from the Duke and Duchess of Cambridge to David Beckham wanted to see the gentlemen's quarter-finals – one of the most splendid entries on the Royal Box list read "Grylls – Mr and Mrs Bear", leaving us to wonder how the intrepid adventurer had managed to abseil into the All England Club while wrestling a crocodile and without anyone noticing.

Meanwhile, Hollywood star Bradley Cooper was invited as Roger Federer's guest on No.1 Court. The *American Sniper* was grateful that his friend disposed of Gilles Simon's challenge so quickly that he had plenty of time to get back to the Theatre Royal. One minute he was with all the beautiful people and the next preparing for another night as the *Elephant Man* in the West End.

- **It was good to hear** three-time finalist Andy Roddick's one-liners back at Wimbledon in his new capacity as a BBC analyst. Asked if he had met British sporting icon David Beckham before, the American couldn't resist joking: "No, but I have long been an admirer of his hair."

- **A most popular innovation** for players at The Championships were the new ice baths, great for post-match recovery but also pretty welcome as a general escape from the sweltering temperatures.

While Andy Murray was being numbly reinvigorated in the bath following his victory over Vasek Pospisil, the boxing fan got a surprise visitor, fellow British Olympic champion and now professional heavyweight superstar, Anthony Joshua.

It was a sight to make anyone freeze. "He's not a scary guy when you meet him but when you see him in the ring, he can do a lot of damage," said Murray. "I certainly wouldn't want to get on the wrong side of him!"

- **The adventures of Duck Hee Lee**, the Korean teenager who has overcome his lifelong deafness to become a top prospect, were finally ended in the last 16 of the boys' singles when he was well beaten by Finland's Patrik Niklas-Salminen.

It concluded another wonderful experience for the 17-year-old who has won so many admirers for his pioneering efforts. Lee can only hear vibrations but not line calls nor the umpire's voice, so had to rely on hand gestures from two courtside aids to help him clarify whether the ball was in or out.

Djokovic, a fan of the youngster's positive attitude, took time out to watch Lee's second-round win and even invited the youngster to have a hit with him to warm up for his fourth-round match against Kevin Anderson.

"His story and ability to overcome his obstacles is something that can bring hope to a lot of people," said the impressed champ.

Duck Hee Lee's memorable Championships included the chance to practise with an admiring Novak Djokovic

DAY TEN
THURSDAY 9 JULY

Any player who can beat Serena Williams at a Grand Slam tournament, as Garbine Muguruza did at the 2014 French Open, deserves respect. However, at the start of The Championships 2015 would anyone have given the 21-year-old Spaniard a chance of making the final? It would have taken a brave pundit to tip Muguruza, who for all her promise on clay and hard courts had barely made any impact on grass. In her two grass court tournaments going into The Championships she had lost to Magdalena Rybarikova (world No.59) and Jo Konta (world No.146) and won only one match, against Polona Hercog (world No.81). In her two previous appearances at the All England Club Muguruza had won just once, beating Britain's Anne Keothavong, then the world No.217, in 2013.

Garbine Muguruza
(above) *surpassed*
one of the best
grass court
tacticians there is

Come semi-final day, however, the world No.20 was still going strong. Having negotiated tricky opening rounds against Varvara Lepchenko and Mirjana Lucic-Baroni, Muguruza had reached the last four by beating three higher-ranked opponents in Angelique Kerber, Caroline Wozniacki and Timea Bacsinszky. Now came an even tougher test against Agnieszka Radwanska, a former junior champion who had lost to Williams so narrowly in the 2012 final and was playing in her third semi-final at The Championships in four years. Having had a shaky start to the year during a brief spell when she had been coached by Martina Navratilova, Radwanska had turned her season around on grass, her run at the All England Club having followed appearances in the semi-finals at Nottingham and the final at Eastbourne.

However, if Radwanska had hoped her less experienced opponent might suffer with nerves she was soon to be disappointed. Muguruza hit the ball cleanly from the start and took the first set in just 34 minutes. When she went 3-1 up in the second it seemed that a swift finish might be in sight, but Radwanska suddenly found her rhythm. Pulling Muguruza around the court, the former world No.2 cut the flow of thumping ground-stroke winners from her opponent's racket. Winning six games in a row to level the match and make an early break in the decider, Radwanska seemed to have turned the contest around, only for Muguruza to force a final change of momentum.

Radwanska went 5-2 down, held serve to stay in the match and then saw some nerves finally creep into Muguruza's game as she served for a place in the final. At deuce, however, Radwanska made a crucial error when she stopped mid-rally to challenge after cries of "out" from the direction of her player box following a deep shot from Muguruza. Hawk-Eye's cameras showed the ball had clipped the baseline and Muguruza went on to complete a 6-2, 3-6, 6-3 victory with a winning volley. "It was a 50-50 decision but it wasn't a very good decision," Radwanska said afterwards.

Agnieszka Radwanska mounted a gutsy fightback

Muguruza was the first Spanish woman to reach the final since Arantxa Sanchez-Vicario in 1996. She had chosen to represent Spain rather than Venezuela only at the end of 2014. Born in Venezuela, she has a Venezuelan mother and Spanish father. The family moved to Barcelona when she was six. Within two years she was playing tennis at an academy run by the former French Open champion, Sergi Bruguera. Muguruza started appearing regularly on the main tour in 2012 and won her first — and to this point only – title in Hobart in 2014. The Spaniard takes full advantage of her 6ft frame to hit the ball with great power, on both her serve and ground strokes, but also moves smoothly around the court. Asked about the improvements she had made in the last two years, she said: "I've grown so much mentally. I'm tougher now. Technically I've also improved a lot. In two years you have a lot of time to improve a lot of things. I've also learned how to play on grass."

Muguruza endeared herself to the Centre Court crowd

The crowd had quickly warmed to Muguruza's elegant style, engaging smile and evident sense of humour. Off the court she enjoys cooking, particularly when given the opportunity to indulge her sweet tooth, and revealed that she had been spending time in the kitchen during The Championships. "Now that I'm here in Wimbledon in the house I sometimes like doing the dessert," she said. "I know it's not good for me, but it's how I like to spend time."

Muguruza and Radwanska were followed on to Centre Court by two players who had met in the final 11 years earlier. Maria Sharapova, who was

only 17 at the time, had beaten Serena Williams in one of the most memorable finals in history. The Russian had gone on to achieve much in the sport, including a "career Grand Slam" of the four major titles, but after getting the better of Williams again in the 2004 end-of-season WTA Finals had lost to the American 16 times in a row. In their previous 12 encounters Sharapova had won just one set.

A number of those matches had been closely fought, but this was a one-sided affair. Williams won 6-2, 6-4, hit 13 aces to Sharapova's two, struck 29 winners to Sharapova's nine and did not face a break point. The writing was on the wall for Sharapova from the moment she was broken in the opening game after double-faulting three times. Asked afterwards what she had to do to be more competitive against Williams, Sharapova said: "A lot more than I'm doing." The Russian was in no mood to respond to a question about a grunting joke made that morning by David Cameron, the British Prime Minister, at a Downing Street reception to celebrate the performances of the England women's football team at the World Cup. When asked for her thoughts about Mr Cameron's advice to the footballers to take their ear plugs when they went to the All England Club later in the day, Sharapova replied: "Next question please."

Williams, meanwhile, had played with a freedom that spoke of her ability to shut out thoughts of the possible milestones that lay ahead. She was going for her sixth singles title at the All England Club, her 21st at Grand Slam level and her second "Serena Slam" of the four major titles in succession but not in the same calendar year. "I've won so many Grand Slam titles," Williams said. "I'm in a position where I don't need to win another Wimbledon. I could lose [on Saturday]. Sure, I won't be happy, but I don't need another Wimbledon title. I don't need another US Open. I don't need any titles to make it. Every time I step out on court, the practice court, the match court, I do look at it as a more fun time because it's not as stressful as it was."

Maria Sharapova had no answer to Serena Williams in their 20th meeting. Williams outplayed her great rival in every facet of her game

Jamie Murray and John Peers reached their first Grand Slam final as a team when they beat Jonathan Erlich and Philipp Petzschner 4-6, 6-3, 6-4, 6-2 in the Gentlemen's Doubles Championship. Erlich and Petzschner were carrying injuries and Murray and Peers were quick to take advantage. The Centre Court crowd reserved one of their biggest cheers for a smart catch by David Beckham when a ball flew up into the Royal Box.

The reward for Murray and Peers would be a return to Centre Court to face Jean-Julien Rojer and Horia Tecau, who beat Rohan Bopanna and Florin Mergea 4-6, 6-2, 6-3, 4-6, 13-11. With his brother

Catch Of The Day!

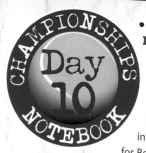

CHAMPIONSHIPS Day 10 NOTEBOOK

• **What is it about David Beckham?** Even when tucked away quietly in the Royal Box, he cannot help being the centre of attention.

While he was supporting Jamie Murray in his doubles semi-final, the ball flew off a line judge's chair, shot into the air towards the Royal Box only for Beckham to take a comfortable one-handed catch. Cue a delay to proceedings as the crowd broke into wild applause and Becks looked wonderfully sheepish.

• **The gregarious Nick Bollettieri,** *eminence grise* of tennis coaching, made the delightful admission that he was so enamoured with the ambience on The Hill that he'd actually rather watch a game with the fans there than on Centre Court itself.

"I love Henman Hill, Murray Mound, whatever you call it. Sitting up there is better than sitting inside the court," wrote Bollettieri in his delightfully blunt *Independent* newspaper column. "You can talk and bulls***, there's no 'quiet please', everyone is yakking away and drinking their wine, beer and Pimm's."

• **You don't have to see Wimbledon** to discover what a magnificent event it is. You only have to hear it.

Crowds crossing the bridge in the Queue were being put in the mood every day by a brilliant three-minute 'soundscape' installation created by artist Louise Brown and her recording partner Rick Blything. As part of the Wimbledon Learning Department's increasingly popular Community Art Project, youngsters from Wandsworth Vision Support Service also joined in to help create the iconic sounds of Wimbledon using 'non-tennis related objects'. Incredibly, they achieved the desired result using items like a microwave oven, leather gloves, peaches, elastic bands and a 2-metre length of metal pipe.

So, for instance, that wasn't a ball bouncing on the grass you heard but a kiwi fruit falling onto a bed of coriander. And that tennis racket you thought Federer was swishing so elegantly? It was a lad swinging the inner tube of a bicycle.

• **The best job at Wimbledon?** Jonathan Parker, head of catering at Wimbledon, revealed that every morning, after more than 100,000 strawberries were picked at 4.30am at a farm in Kent, packaged and sent fresh to the All England Club, he had the labour of love of sampling them for breakfast to check their quality. His verdict so far? "Well, everyone's telling me they're a really good crop this year, better than ever – and I have to say I agree!"

The strawberries were said to be particularly delicious in 2015

WIMBLEDON IN NUMBERS

11 Years since Maria Sharapova last beat Serena Williams, at the WTA Finals in 2004

Andy facing Roger Federer in the semi-finals of the Gentlemen's Singles Championship the following day – and with the possibility of Novak Djokovic awaiting in the final – Murray was asked whether a family double might be on the cards. "Well, he's got to beat Federer and maybe Djokovic," Jamie said. "We have to beat Rojer and Tecau. I'd probably rather be us than him, I think."

Martina Hingis kept alive her hopes of playing in two finals when she partnered Leander Paes to a 6-2, 6-1 quarter-final victory over Marcin Matkowski and Elena Vesnina in the Mixed Doubles Championship. Alexander Peya and Timea Babos beat the No.2 seeds, Bruno Soares and Sania Mirza, 3-6, 7-6(6), 9-7.

Taylor Fritz, the No.1 seed in the boys' singles, dropped his first set of the week before beating Yunseong Chung 6-2, 4-6, 6-0 to earn a semi-final meeting with his fellow American, Reilly Opelka, who beat William Blumberg 6-3, 6-3. Patrik Niklas-Salminen beat Tommy Paul, the French Open champion, 6-4, 1-6, 6-4, while Mikael Ymer beat Alvaro Lopez San Martin 7-5, 7-6(3). With Britain's Katie Swan losing 6-7(2), 0-6 to Viktoria Kuzmova after taking an injury time-out in the second set, Anna Blinkova was the only seed to reach the semi-finals of the girls' singles. The Russian beat Tornado Alicia Black 1-6, 6-3, 12-10 after more than three hours on court.

Jamie Murray and doubles partner John Peers advanced to the final

HAPPY AS MURRAY!

Andy Murray had said before Wimbledon that he had never felt happier nor more relaxed going into The Championships. This was demonstrated during the Fortnight as, injury-free and working contentedly with his support team led by laid-back coach Amelie Mauresmo, a smile never seemed far from his face. An idea of his cheery mood could be gleaned from one of the most popular videos on wimbledon.com, showing a chuckling Murray helping train some Cocker Spaniel pups to become sniffer dogs for the Metropolitan Police. And if it wasn't Andy beaming, it was his fans wearing the now must-have items – those smiley Murray masks.

DAY ELEVEN
FRIDAY 11 JULY

R oger Federer has probably faced the same question at post-match press conferences more times than any player in history: "Was that your greatest ever performance?" In giving his response, which he always does with the utmost respect to the questioner, Federer sometimes shrugs his shoulders before explaining that he finds it impossible to make such judgements. In recent years the question has been asked less frequently, but it was first on the agenda after a breath-taking victory over Andy Murray sent the 33-year-old Swiss into his 10th final in the Gentlemen's Singles Championship, extending his own Open era record. "The thing is you can't compare different days, different opponents, different surfaces," Federer said after his 7-5, 7-5, 6-4 triumph. "But it was definitely one of the best matches I've played in my career."

Roger Federer was always on the front foot in the Centre Court sunshine

For a player who had won only one Grand Slam title in the previous five years, when he beat Murray in the final of The Championships 2012, Federer's display was simply stunning. There might have been times earlier in his career when he had played better, but Greg Rusedski was among those who doubted it. "I am struggling to remember a better performance by Federer, even in his 2004/05 vintage," the former world No.4 wrote in the *Daily Telegraph* the following day. Yet this was a man who was being written off at the end of 2013 after a season in which he had won only one minor title, which was his worst haul for 12 years. He came back, nevertheless, the following year and reached his ninth final at The Championships before losing a thriller to Novak Djokovic. Now he was proving that his excellent 2014 had been much more than a mere late flicker of a dying light.

Everything about Federer's game was in great shape, from his thunderbolt forehand to his majestic backhand, from his sharp volleys to his speed around the court. Best of all was his serve, which is sometimes overlooked in assessments of his greatest attributes. Federer cannot match the serving power of some of his rivals – even on this occasion his average first-serve speed was 1mph slower than Murray's at 118mph – but opponents find it almost impossible to read where he is going to place the ball. On a beautiful summer's afternoon, in near-perfect conditions, 76 per cent of Federer's first serves found the target. Murray, who is one of the best returners in the game, won only 11 out of 69 points on Federer's first serve. Federer's second serve was also relentlessly accurate. Crucially, at 100mph it was an average 11mph faster than Murray's. The Scot said afterwards that Federer had never served better against him. Murray struggled to attack Federer's second serve, while the Swiss was ruthless in going for his opponent's.

Federer had 10 break points and converted three of them. Murray had only one, in the very first game, which Federer saved with an unreturned serve. It was not as if Murray played poorly. The world No.3 defended with his usual athleticism and countered Federer's regular assaults on the net with some excellent passing shots and lobs, but the Swiss was irresistible. Federer had plenty of support, as he always does on Centre Court, but it was often Murray who got the crowd going as he fist-pumped in celebration of his best shots. However, all three sets followed a similar pattern, with Murray clinging on to his serve, Federer holding on to his more comfortably and then turning up the pressure when the Scot needed to hold to keep the set or match alive.

For Murray the result was at least a major improvement on his previous meeting with Federer, who had dropped only one game in winning their round-robin match at the Barclays ATP World Tour Finals in London eight months earlier. Murray thought he had served better than at any stage of the Fortnight but wondered whether he could have done more with his first-serve returns. "I don't feel like I played that badly," he said. "He served fantastic, apart from the first game where I had the chance there. Then that puts pressure on you. The pressure builds throughout the set."

Andy Murray admitted that there was little he could do to keep up with Roger Federer during their semi-final

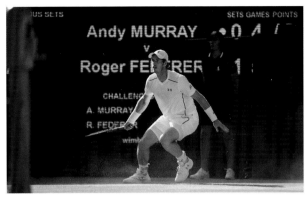

Federer was in as sublime form as he has ever been at Wimbledon, serving particularly superbly. And despite giving it everything he had, Murray was unable to upset his rhythm

Did Federer think his performance had been the perfect answer to those who, not so long ago, questioned why he was continuing to play? "I think the fans know why I'm playing," he said. "At the end of the day, I enjoy it. I work hard in practice. In a match like this, I can have a great performance. And clearly it's an amazing feeling when you come back from the match and everybody's so happy for you. Even like on the inside of the Royal Box when I was walking back, there was applause all the way to the locker room – something I don't remember really having, except maybe on one of the wins I've had here."

Earlier in the day Djokovic had secured his place in the final for the fourth time in five years by beating Richard Gasquet 7-6(2), 6-4, 6-4. Gasquet competed well for most of the first set, only to undermine his good work by playing a poor tie-break. Djokovic looked more comfortable thereafter and went on to secure his 12th victory in 13 meetings with the Frenchman. Djokovic's only concern was a stiff left shoulder for which he had treatment, though he insisted it would not be a problem for the final.

"The first set was really close," Djokovic said. "I thought Richard played some really good tennis, especially from the backhand side. It was really difficult for me at times to play any kind of ball to his backhand side because he was really going for it, especially along the line. He made a lot of winners. He used the chipped backhand slice variety as well. It was very close, but that was probably the turning point. Winning the first set tie-break was psychologically very helpful for the rest of the match."

Gasquet acknowledged the quality of Djokovic's returns of serve. "He never misses a return," the world No.20 said. "You serve and the ball always comes back on your side. It's very difficult. You never make so many aces. He doesn't make unforced errors. Even from the baseline he's playing fast with a lot of aggressivity. He takes the ball early. That's why it's tough."

To the despair of fans on The Hill **(above)**, *Federer swept past Murray in three sets*

(Opposite page) *Earlier in the day, Novak Djokovic had brushed past Richard Gasquet*

At times the spectacular Serb's all-action, swashbuckling style reminded the Centre Court crowd of a certain former Wimbledon winner turned coach who was now sitting on the reigning champion's side of the players' box

12

Years since
Roger Federer
reached his first
Wimbledon singles final

Seventeen years after playing in her last final at The Championships, Martina Hingis secured her passage into two more with victories in the semi-finals of both the Ladies' Doubles Championship and the Mixed Doubles Championship. Hingis and Sania Mirza beat Raquel Kops-Jones and Abigail Spears 6-1, 6-2 in the ladies' doubles to book a

Martina Hingis advanced to two Grand Slam finals

place in the final against Ekaterina Makarova and Elena Vesnina, who beat Timea Babos and Kristina Mladenovic 6-3, 4-6, 6-4. In the mixed event Hingis teamed up with Leander Paes to beat Mike Bryan and Bethanie Mattek-Sands, the No.1 seeds, 6-3, 6-4 and set up a final against Alexander Peya and Babos, who beat Robert Lindstedt and Annabel Medina Garrigues 4-6, 6-3, 11-9.

"It's more than I could have dreamed of when I started this journey," Hingis said. "It's different now. Obviously I was enjoying winning when I was 16, 17. It was just more stressful. You didn't have much time to celebrate this because there is next week and you keep being the hunted one. In doubles the practice is not as much or as physical as it was for singles. For singles I used to practise six hours a day. Now it's probably only two or three."

Hingis, who won the ladies' doubles at The Championships in 1996 with Helena Sukova and in 1998 with Jana Novotna, only got together with Mirza in March. However, the partnership clicked immediately and after they won titles in Indian Wells, Miami and Charleston, Mirza became the first Indian woman ever to reach No.1 in the world rankings.

17-year-old Reilly Opelka reached the boys' singles final

The unseeded Reilly Opelka, who stands at 6 foot 10 inches at the age of just 17, hit 18 aces past Taylor Fritz, a fellow American, to reach the final of the boys' singles. Opelka won 6-3, 7-6(13) after a hard-fought second set. Opelka let slip a 5-0 lead in the tie-break but eventually won it 15-13. Sweden's Mikael Ymer sent for the trainer and doctor after feeling dizzy before the other semi-final, but recovered to beat Finland's Patrik Niklas-Salminen 7-6(3), 6-3. Two Russians won the girls' semi-finals. Anna Blinkova, the No.12 seed, beat Vera Lapko 6-2, 7-6(1), while Sofya Zhuk beat Viktoria Kuzmova 6-1, 6-3.

Bjorn Again

• **Five-times champion** Bjorn Borg, always a welcome visitor to Wimbledon and still looking impossibly youthful for a man in his 60th year, smiled after taking his place in the front row of the Royal Box on Centre Court to watch the gentlemen's semi-finals: "I can't complain about my seat," he said.

The Swede, whose clothes business is thriving, reckoned he was happiest these days spending time with his family, and he takes a close interest in his 12-year-old son Leo's burgeoning progress on the courts.

So, what kind of tennis parent is Bjorn, who was always the model of calm during his career? "Oh, I'm one of the nicer, good ones, not one of those who's completely crazy," he explained to his old friend and compatriot Mats Wilander on Live @ Wimbledon.

"Leo plays with Max Bjorkman, Jonas's son. Me and Jonas, we stay on the side and are nice and loose. But some parents can be crazy in tennis and that's why they destroy some of their own kids."

• **The presence of the great** Rod Laver, back in the Royal Box for gentlemen's semi-final day, was a delight for everyone at this Wimbledon, leaving some of the best players of all time a little starstruck when in his company.

As Andy Roddick put it splendidly: "Even McEnroe, when he's around Rod Laver, it's like a 13-year-old girl at a Justin Bieber concert!"

• **Martyn Falconer,** Wimbledon's head gardener, sounded rightly proud of the work he had overseen in creating the feel of "tennis in an English garden" in the Grounds, with its blooming bee friendly pollinators, its natural wild flowers theme and beautiful displays of foxgloves, lupins and the like.

Presumably, it was put to him, his garden at home must be something to behold too? "Err, no, my garden doesn't look this good," smiled Martyn. "I spend a lot more time here – and I don't have 12 guys looking after my garden from 6 o'clock in the morning!"

• **Britain's Jordanne Whiley** moved to within one match of successfully defending her wheelchair ladies' doubles title with Japan's Yui Kamiji after a straight-sets victory over Louise Hunt and Katharina Kruger in the semi-finals.

It was another performance to elevate 23-year-old Whiley's sporting profile in Britain, even though she admitted she hadn't quite been able to get used to her rapid rise.

Indeed, when an official-looking letter dropped on her doormat in the build-up to Wimbledon informing her that she was going to be made a Member of the British Empire in the Queen's Birthday Honours list, she admitted that she thought she must be getting a parking fine, not an MBE!

British wheelchair tennis star, Jordanne Whiley in action

DAY TWELVE
SATURDAY 11 JULY

F or weeks the media talk had been of the Grand Slam and the "Serena Slam", of overtaking Steffi Graf and Margaret Court, of going down in the record books as the greatest player in history. Serena Williams, however, had only one goal in mind. "I just knew I wanted to win Wimbledon this year," the world No.1 said after lifting the Venus Rosewater Dish for the sixth time. "That's how I got through this. It wasn't about winning the 'Serena Slam'. It was about winning Wimbledon. I hadn't won here in a while and I really wanted to win this title."

Serena Williams and Garbine Muguruza took the traditional walk to Centre Court

Williams has not achieved her myriad successes by concerning herself with records and milestones. At heart the 33-year-old American is a ferocious competitor who just loves winning matches and titles. It was her refusal to be beaten that had seen her battle through sickness to win the French Open the previous month and come through her biggest challenges at The Championships, most notably a third-round encounter with Heather Watson in which she had gone within two points of defeat.

Going into the final against Garbine Muguruza, Williams knew she had to focus on the task in hand. The 21-year-old Spaniard had inflicted the heaviest defeat on Williams in her 318-match Grand Slam career with her 6-2, 6-2 victory at the French Open in 2014 and had taken a set off her in their only subsequent meeting at the 2015 Australian Open. On grass Muguruza had come of age at The Championships to reach her first Grand Slam final.

If there were any nerves at the start they appeared to be on Williams' side of the net as she dropped her serve in the opening game after three double faults. Muguruza, hitting her big ground strokes with confidence, went 2-0 up. When Williams went 0-30 down in the third game she screamed in frustration. The crowd had quickly taken to Muguruza and as the Spaniard went 3-1 up there was an air of excitement around Centre Court.

At 4-3, however, Williams broke back and the momentum quickly shifted. As Muguruza started to make mistakes, Williams struck the ball with greater confidence and took the first set. By the time she had broken to go 5-1 up in the second set Williams had won nine of the previous 10 games. It was a complete turnaround, but just when Muguruza's challenge appeared to be collapsing she launched a fightback. As Muguruza went for broke Williams twice failed to serve out for the match, with even the American joining in the applause at one moment as the Spaniard cracked a thunderous winning backhand cross-court pass. Muguruza saved a match point at 5-3, but in the following game she went 0-40 down and then missed a forehand to give Williams victory. The crowd showed their appreciation for the runner-up at the presentation ceremony with a lengthy

The Central Band of The Royal British Legion, under the direction of Captain David Cole MVO, warmed up the crowd on Centre Court

standing ovation. "I couldn't stop crying," Muguruza said later. "So many people were clapping. I had made all these people feel this in a tennis court? I felt special."

At 33 years and 289 days Williams was the oldest Grand Slam champion of the modern era. She won her 21st Grand Slam title 16 years after her first; when Williams won the US Open in 1999 Muguruza was just five years old. Of all Williams' many achievements, her success in her later years is possibly the most extraordinary. Since Patrick Mouratoglou became her coach in 2012, when she was 30, Williams had won eight of the 13 Grand Slam tournaments she had contested. Her sixth Wimbledon title, which came three years after her fifth, took her one ahead of her sister Venus.

The term "Serena Slam" – to denote holding all four Grand Slam trophies at the same time but not in the same calendar year – had been coined in 2003, when Williams added the Australian Open to the French, Wimbledon and US titles which she had already won. Now she held all four major titles again. "I honestly wouldn't have thought last year after winning the US Open that I would win the 'Serena Slam' at all," she said. "It's super exciting."

Now Williams knew that victory at the US Open later in the summer would complete her first pure calendar-year singles Grand Slam, which had been performed by only three women in history – by Maureen Connolly in 1953, by Court in 1970 and by Graf in 1988. Victory in New York would also see Williams equal Graf's Open era record of 22 Grand Slam singles titles and move within two of Court's all-time mark. However, the world No.1 said she would not be spending the next seven weeks discussing such feats. "You'd better ask all your questions about the Grand Slam because it will be banned soon," she told a small group of reporters a few hours after

The coin toss was performed by Kaci Finch of the Wimbledon Junior Tennis Initiative

Garbine Muguruza put Serena Williams through her paces in a final that was far closer than the scoreline indicated

Ultimately, Serena proved superior, jumping for joy as she won her sixth Wimbledon singles title

3.36 ♕ ROLEX ♕ 1.23

PREV SETS

SETS GAMES POINTS

6 Serena WILLIAMS 2 6

v

4 Garbine MUGURUZA 0 4

CHALLENGES REMAINING

S. WILLIAMS 3

G. MUGURUZA 1

wimbledon.com

While Muguruza wept at the overwhelming occasion, Serena could hardly contain her joy, joking with Sue Barker and waving the trophy around in delight

her victory. "I'm really nice right now, but sooner or later it's going to be cut out because I can't think about that. I have to go into New York thinking: 'Listen, I want to win the US Open. I want to defend my title. And that's the only reason I want to be there'."

When Williams beat Martina Hingis to win her maiden Grand Slam trophy at the 1999 US Open, it would have been hard to imagine that both women would win Wimbledon titles on the same day 16 years later. Hingis, however, took to Centre Court later in the afternoon and won the Ladies' Doubles Championship with her partner, Sania Mirza, after a thrilling final against the Russians Ekaterina Makarova and Elena Vesnina. The 34-year-old Swiss and the 28-year-old Indian won 5-7, 7-6(4), 7-5, having trailed 5-2 in the deciding set. The players left the court at 5-5 in the decider because of fading light but returned after the roof had been closed, allowing the match to be completed under lights. Hingis served out to complete her third ladies' doubles triumph at The Championships following her successes in 1996 (with Helena Sukova) and 1998 (with Jana Novotna). "It feels like it was in another life," Hingis said as she thought back to that 1998 success, which was her last in any competition at the All England Club. Having won five Grand Slam singles titles in the 1990s, Hingis retired because of injuries in 2002 before returning in 2006, only to retire again the following year. She came back for a second time in 2013 to play doubles.

Mirza, who had never previously won a Grand Slam title in ladies' doubles, said of her partnership with Hingis: "We complement each other's games. She's really solid around the net and I try and put in the power. That's how we really combine well. Our temperaments match on the court as well. We try and have fun as much as we can, obviously, at this level but as competitors we suit each other. We just go out there and try to treat it like any other match."

Serena took the trophy for the customary celebration on the Members' Balcony, while Sania Mirza and Martina Hingis (right) were jumping for joy a little later after winning the ladies' doubles

The Dutchman Jean-Julien Rojer and the Romanian Horia Tecau, playing in their first Grand Slam final as a pair, won the Gentlemen's Doubles Championship, beating Britain's Jamie Murray and Australia's John Peers 7-6(5), 6-4, 6-4. Tecau, who was runner-up in 2010, 2011 and 2012 alongside Robin Lindstedt, avoided becoming

Jamie Murray and John Peers (above) were outplayed by Jean-Julien Rojer and Horia Tecau in the men's doubles final (below)

only the second player in the professional era, after Stan Smith, to lose his first four Wimbledon finals. It had been quite a fortnight for the No.4 seeds, who won marathon fifth sets against Andre Begemann and Julian Knowle (15-13 in the second round) and against Rohan Bopanna and Florin Mergea (13-11 in the semi-finals).

Murray and Peers, who were also appearing in their first final as a team, were left to regret their failure to convert any of their three break points in the first set, while single breaks of serve in the second and third sets proved costly. Murray's brother, Andy, gave loud support from the stands, but to no avail. Jamie said it had been "a missed opportunity" for himself and Peers but added: "It was a good tournament for us. We got to the final of Wimbledon, which is not so easy to do."

The unseeded Sofya Zhuk, aged 15, won the girls' singles title, beating her fellow Russian Anna Blinkova 7-5, 6-4. Zhuk, who is based at Justine Henin's academy in Belgium, made early breaks in both sets and was grateful the match did not go to a decider. "In the middle of the second set I started to have a lot of cramping in my calves," she said afterwards. "I was trying to stay focused because I knew that if I had lost the second set I would not be able to play the third."

OH BROTHER!

Suddenly, we remembered why Andy Murray rarely goes courtside to watch Jamie's doubles matches. Andy had come to believe he was a jinx whenever he turned up to support big brother but overcame his superstitious nature to cheer him and John Peers in the Gentlemen's Doubles final. Watching Andy shouting, gesticulating and evidently writhing through all kinds of agonies proved almost as diverting as the match itself. Alas, though, his vocal support came in a losing cause and it was obvious he'd rather have been out there playing alongside Jamie. A week after Wimbledon, he did just that, the brothers-in-arms combining for victory against France in the Davis Cup.

IT'S BEEN A WHILE

Martina Hingis (left) celebrates her first Wimbledon title for 17 years. She had previously won the ladies' doubles title in 1996, the singles in 1997, and the doubles again in 1998

When Martina Hingis last won a Wimbledon title, she laughed, it was like another lifetime ago in another world. After 17 years – actually, half a lifetime in her case – that's just how it felt to everyone cheering her 'double doubles' triumph on Centre Court.

Was it really THAT long ago, we had to pinch ourselves? When she was the original 'Swiss Miss' phenomenon back in 1998, odd things called DVDs had just hit the shops in Tony Blair's Britain, *Titanic* was keeping the film industry buoyant,

President Clinton was embroiled in a sex scandal and David Beckham was England's public enemy No.1 after being sent off at the World Cup.

Hingis's victory with Jana Novotna, who had dethroned her as singles champion in the semi-finals that same year, came the same day that Pete Sampras won the gentlemen's singles title, a week before Michael Schumacher was to win the British Grand Prix and a day after Dennis

Bergkamp's genius goal for Netherlands knocked Argentina out of the World Cup. Yes, that long ago…

Still, after all these years, something hasn't changed. Hingis may have endured injury woes, anti-climax and even a drugs scandal since those days when she had looked ready to be tennis's queen for years to come. Yet on this glorious weekend, her old beaming countenance illuminated SW19 just as it had when she became Wimbledon's youngest singles champion in 1997 and was hailed by the *New York Times* as having the "the smile of a cheerleader and the appetite of a shark".

Now, the happy Great White was back, giving a fine impression of still being the world's best doubles player with those lovely volleys, pinpoint ground strokes and intelligent court craft as she joined forces with her Indian friends, Sania Mirza and Leander Paes, to take her tally of all Grand Slam triumphs to 18.

The smile just wouldn't evaporate. And that fantastic comeback win with Mirza under a floodlit, enclosed Centre Court? "We didn't even have a roof back in the day!" she couldn't resist reminding us all.

Just Did It!

• **Not only did she prove herself** to be the best tennis player in the world again, but Serena Williams also demonstrated in her post-final conference why she must be a sponsor's dream.

Asked what she felt the toughest thing to accomplish in her record-breaking career was, Williams cited how difficult it was to "stay in the moment and do your best". And when the reporter persisted — "How do you do that?" — Williams responded, quick as a flash: "Just do it!" You could almost picture her sponsors at Nike giving each other high fives.

• **After Williams's triumph,** her inspirational coach Patrick Mouratoglou gave an insight into the training that he believes keeps her ahead of the pack.

"Maybe she's doing a bit more these days, not in terms of quantity but quality," the Frenchman told Live @ Wimbledon. "She's not there for long but trains with an intensity that's really something you can compare with Rafa [Nadal] on the men's side. That's what makes her Serena Williams."

• **Sania Mirza,** India's first-ever ladies' Wimbledon champion, was a nation's darling after partnering Martina Hingis to an historic victory in the Ladies' Doubles Championship.

Mumbai's heroine Mirza, a trailblazer for women's sport back home, was flooded with messages of congratulations from all over the country, including not just the greatest of all Indian sportsmen, cricketer Sachin Tendulkar, but also Bollywood superstars like Shah Rukh Khan and even the Prime Minister, Narendra Modi.

And Mirza herself reckoned the support at Wimbledon had made her feel as if this were a home from home. "There are so many Indians in England, I've always had amazing support here especially," she beamed. "I think for me as an Indian, I'm in Little India here!"

• **It was the start of an emotional weekend** for the popular Jenny Higgs, who was retiring as Chief Umpire 50 years after she first officiated at Wimbledon.

As she oversaw her last weekend organising all the officials for the finals in her 44th Championships, some happy memories flooded back for the 68-year-old Briton.

Surrounded now by a sophisticated computer operation, she remembers when she was first asked to do the chief umpiring job at Roehampton qualifying in 1990 and she introduced a new system of allocating umpiring assignments. "I used colour-coded clothes pegs — I've still got them at home!" she recalls. "We've come a long way since then."

Jenny's finest hour? She remembers Steffi Graf once having an embarrassing wardrobe malfunction with her skirt on court, but, luckily, this was the woman umpire with the reputation of being able to rescue any situation. "Somehow, I managed to produce a safety pin from behind my lapel," she laughed, recalling how she spared the blushes of the grateful German champion.

Chief Umpire Jenny Higgs is hanging up her baton this year

uth West Hall

DAY THIRTEEN
SUNDAY 12 JULY

There is always something particularly pleasing about the meeting of the No.1 and No.2 seeds in a Wimbledon final. However much excitement might be generated by the emergence of new talent – or even by the late blossoming of a more experienced campaigner – it seems fitting for the very best players to bestride the biggest stage of all. The seedings and the world rankings do not lie. Despite the resurgence of Andy Murray and Stan Wawrinka's late arrival among the elite, Novak Djokovic and Roger Federer were clearly the best two players in men's tennis, especially on grass. They were contesting the final of the Gentlemen's Singles Championship for the second year in a row. To have an idea of how history might look back on them, just consider the other pairs of players who had played in successive finals at The Championships in the Open era: Bjorn Borg and Jimmy Connors; Borg and John McEnroe; Stefan Edberg and Boris Becker; Federer and Andy Roddick; Federer and Rafael Nadal.

Roger Federer (above) took an early lead against Novak Djokovic in overcast conditions

One question above all others hung over the 2015 final. Could Federer maintain the stunning form he had shown in beating Murray in the semi-finals? He would surely need to given Djokovic's excellence since the start of the year. Over the Wimbledon Fortnight he had looked every inch the world No.1, with the exception of the first two sets he lost to Kevin Anderson in the fourth round.

Federer, relishing the speed with which the balls had flown through the air and off the court, had thrived in the Fortnight's glorious warm weather, but on Day 13 it was cooler and overcast. The conditions were more likely to favour Djokovic, though there was speculation that the rain forecast for mid-afternoon could be in Federer's favour. Nobody plays better indoors than the 33-year-old Swiss, who had benefited three years previously when the Centre Court roof was closed in the middle of the final against Murray.

For all the respect in which Djokovic is held, there was no doubt that many in the crowd were hoping to witness history as Federer attempted to become the first man to win the title eight times. Federer won the opening game to love and the excitement around Centre Court grew five games later when he went 4-2 up as Djokovic, looking ill at ease, netted a backhand at 0-40. However in the next game Federer went 15-40 down – the first time in the Fortnight that he had faced two break points in a row – and Djokovic broke back. Federer had two set points when Djokovic served at 5-6, but the Serb saved both with unreturned serves. Djokovic dominated the subsequent tie-break, which ended with Federer double-faulting at 1-6.

There were only four break points in the second set – three for Federer and one for Djokovic – but none were taken. Djokovic led 6-3 in the tie-break, but Federer played the next three points superbly. As the tension rose, so did the crowd's volume. On Djokovic's seventh set point, at 10-9 on his own serve, the Serb hit a forehand long. Federer won the next point with a killer forehand return and then took the set with a winning volley. The crowd's roar was probably heard in Basle and Belgrade.

Djokovic, however, was unruffled. Federer saved two break points in the opening game of the third set and when he faced another at 1-1 put what should have been an easy kill beyond the baseline. Two games later the players left the court because of rain. Might the Centre Court roof come to Federer's aid again? No. The rain subsided, the roof stayed open and the match resumed after a break of only 21 minutes.

Djokovic served out for the third set and from 1-2 down in the fourth won five of the last six games. As Federer's mistakes multiplied, his last chance came when Djokovic served at 4-3 and 0-30. Federer had won the first two points with huge returns, but Djokovic calmly served his way out of trouble. In the next game a crushing return took Djokovic to Championship point, which he converted with a forehand winner to complete a 7-6(1), 6-7(10), 6-4, 6-3 victory. Having embraced Federer at the net, Djokovic sank to his knees and, as has become his custom, ate a blade of grass. "I was assured that it's gluten-free," he joked afterwards. "It's not processed, completely organic and natural."

But Djokovic broke back and then comfortably won the tie-break to take the first set

It had been a very good final, but the gap between the two men seemed greater than 12 months previously, when Djokovic won in five sets. This time there was a clear winner of the key battleground between Federer's serve and Djokovic's return. Two days earlier Murray had created only one break point against Federer; Djokovic created 10 and converted four. Federer might not have served as well as he had against Murray, but Djokovic was more effective with his returns. On his own serve, meanwhile, Djokovic looked more secure than Murray had, thanks largely to his more potent second serves.

At the presentation ceremony Federer acknowledged Djokovic's excellence. "Novak played not only great today but for the whole two weeks, plus the year, plus last year, plus the year before that," the Swiss said. Djokovic, having become the only player to beat Rafael Nadal at the French Open and Federer at The Championships, admitted that he had felt "very, very frustrated" after losing the second set. "I knew that I could not let this happen against Roger in the final of Wimbledon because this might be my last chance in the match," he said. "But I managed to regroup and had a little bit more time, especially in the rain delay. That's where I got my thoughts together and went back to the basics and played a really, really good match after that."

Djokovic's performance was all the more praiseworthy given his disappointment five weeks earlier when he had failed to take his best chance yet to win the French Open, which remained the only Grand Slam trophy to elude him. "I was disappointed and heartbroken," he admitted. "But one thing I have learned in sport is to recover fast and to leave things behind me and move on."

It also provided further vindication of Djokovic's appointment of Becker as his coach. "It was not always easy at the beginning," Djokovic admitted. "We weren't always on the same side. That doesn't mean we were arguing or had fights. It was just we didn't yet understand each other. It took five or six months to really create this chemistry, both on and off the court. At the beginning it was important for the two of us to understand each other as people, not just as tennis players."

(Opposite page)
The Centre Court crowd, players' boxes and those on The Hill reacted as Federer came back to take the second set

In the third set the reigning champion took control and his third Wimbledon title was soon in the bag

THE VICTORY MOMENT

A Wimbledon final on Centre Court is one of the best tickets in sport. And 15,000 fortunate fans were there to witness Novak Djokovic's reaction as he claimed his third Wimbledon singles title, defeating Roger Federer in four sets. Djokovic threw back his head and roared, a customary occasion, while Federer could only look bitterly disappointed. After a short break, the trophy presentation ceremony took place under the closed Centre Court roof.

Djokovic celebrated his third Wimbledon title in his usual emphatic fashion as his box rose to their feet

Djokovic saw his victory as a triumph for marriage and fatherhood. Since 1987 Djokovic and Federer have been the only fathers to win the Gentlemen's Singles Championship. Djokovic and Jelena Ristic married in the week after The Championships 2014 and their son, Stefan, was born three months later. "Ever since I got married and became a father, I haven't lost many matches and I won many tournaments," Djokovic said. "I suggest that to every player: get married, have kids, let's enjoy this."

While Federer failed to become the oldest Wimbledon champion in the Open era, Djokovic matched Becker by lifting the Challenge Cup for a third time. Competing as he does against rivals – Federer and Nadal – who have won 17 and 14 Grand Slam titles respectively, Djokovic has yet to receive the acclaim that history will surely bestow on him. He has been the best player on the planet for the best part of five years and by winning his ninth Grand Slam title moved clear of some of the sport's all-time greats in Fred Perry, Ken Rosewall, Jimmy Connors, Ivan Lendl and Andre Agassi. Only seven men have won more Grand Slam titles: Federer (17), Nadal (14), Pete Sampras (14), Roy Emerson (12), Borg (11), Rod Laver (11) and Bill Tilden (10).

The oldest player in the Open era to win his ninth Grand Slam title, Djokovic said he had plenty more to offer. "I'm 28," he said. "I feel good. I don't feel old. I have hopefully many more years in front of me. I'm going to try to push my own limits and see how far I can go."

Proof of the longevity of modern players had come with the traditional finale on Centre Court as Leander Paes, aged 42, and Martina Hingis, aged 34, beat Alexander Peya and Timea Babos 6-1, 6-1 in the final of the Mixed Doubles Championship. Hingis had won her first trophy at The Championships for 17 years the previous day in the ladies' doubles, but had never won the mixed event here. Paes had won the mixed doubles with Lisa Raymond in 1999, Martina Navratilova in 2003 and Cara Black in 2010. Hingis said she had benefited from the confidence derived from her victory 24 hours earlier.

After meeting Federer at the net, (above) the 2015 champion stooped to eat a 'gluten-free' blade of grass (below)

The players took their customary walk of honour around Centre Court, before Djokovic carried the trophy to celebrate on the Members' Balcony

WIMBLEDON IN NUMBERS

76 The combined age of Martina Hingis and Leander Paes, who triumphed in the Mixed Doubles Championship

"Last night and today was just amazing," she said. "The chemistry we had today – it was incredible."

At the other end of the age scale Reilly Opelka, a 17-year-old American, won the boys' singles title, beating Mikael Ymer 7-6(5), 6-4 in the final. Opelka, who was unseeded, used his 6ft 10in frame to power 15 aces past his Swedish opponent. "Every time I felt there could have been a pressure moment, 30-30, 15-30, I came up with an ace or a service winner," he said afterwards.

Opelka went on to partner Akira Santillan in the boys' doubles final, but they were beaten 6-7(4), 4-6 by Nam Hoang Ly and Sumit Nagal. Dalma Galfi and Fanni Stollar won the girls' doubles title, beating Vera Lapko and Tereza Mihalikova 6-3, 6-2 in the final.

Britain's Jordanne Whiley and Japan's Yui Kamiji made a successful defence of their title in the Wheelchair Ladies' Doubles, beating the Dutch pair of Jiske Griffioen and Aniek van Koot 6-2, 5-7, 6-3 in the final. The Argentine-French team of Gustavo Fernandez and Nicolas Peifer won the Wheelchair Gentlemen's Doubles, beating France's Michael Jeremiasz and Britain's Gordon Reid 7-5, 5-7, 6-2. On the 10th anniversary of the introduction of wheelchair tennis at The Championships, the All England Club announced that singles wheelchair events would be introduced in 2016.

At the Champions' Dinner in the Guildhall that evening Djokovic made his own bow to history. In a very different scene to when Borg and Chris Evert danced at the last Champions' Ball in 1976, Djokovic and Serena Williams disco-danced to the Bee Gees' 'Night Fever'. Djokovic explained later that he had suggested a revival of "this tradition which was a bit forgotten" to Philip Brook, the Wimbledon Chairman, and to Williams. "I was very pleased because Serena is a great dancer," Djokovic said. "I was thinking more of a waltz, or something I would say sophisticated, something that would blend into the environment of the beautiful hall where we had the dinner, but Serena wanted to move a little bit more."

It was a fitting way to end another glorious tournament in the chapter of Wimbledon history. Two distinguished champions dancing to their own beat, on the court and off it.

Goran Ivanisevic was his usual exuberant self alongside Ivan Ljubicic in the Invitation Doubles **(below)**

Meanwhile Jordanne Whiley and Yui Kamiji celebrated defending their wheelchair doubles title **(below right)**

Ali In Charge

• **What a great day for Ali Nili,** who did a fine job after being appointed chair umpire for the first time in a Grand Slam singles final. The experience left the proud 37-year-old Iranian-born American hoping he could prove a sporting trailblazer back in his home country. After admitting that he so loved every second of officiating the Novak Djokovic-Roger Federer showdown that he didn't want the experience to end, Nili revealed that he had received a fantastic reaction back in Iran, whose most famous tennis export to date is the exuberant Mansour Bahrami.

"I'm a US citizen but was born in Iran, used to play tennis there and this has become a very big deal for Iranians. People are absolutely delighted there," explained Nili, one of the ATP's 10 full-time umpires.

"We have quite a few tennis fans in Iran and it's nice to see them all being all proud and happy. I represent hope and possibility for the younger generation, showing that with hard work you can achieve basically anything. If they see I did it, umpiring the final of the greatest tennis tournament, then maybe they feel they can achieve what they want too."

• **Inevitably, Federer's defeat** in the final caused widespread deflation among his legion of fans but one admirer, Britain's greatest Olympian, five-time gold medallist Sir Steve Redgrave, had some consoling words for the Swiss master's devotees after watching on Centre Court.

Asked if it was still possible for the 33-year-old to win title number eight, Redgrave responded: "Well, I was 38 when I won my last Olympics. He's got loads of years left yet!"

• **Hingis's double triumph** in two nights was so ecstatically greeted that one mischievous reporter couldn't resist asking her after her mixed doubles victory: "Martina, do you think on Centre Court you are the most popular Swiss – or is it Roger Federer?" To which, as a smiling Hingis kept a diplomatic silence, her doubles partner Leander Paes couldn't help chuckling aloud: "Ooo, it's getting hot in here!"

Reilly Opelka, at 6ft 10in, receives his trophy from the Duke of Kent

• **It was a measure of Federer's class** that, despite obviously feeling raw after his own defeat, he still had time to congratulate giant American youngster Reilly Opelka, winner of the boys' title, in the locker room.

"He was very kind and very gracious, really nice to me, even though he was upset that he lost," Opelka said of the man who himself won the boys' crown in 1998.

This wasn't their first meeting, though. Opelka's dad tweeted a picture of Federer with a beaming nine-year-old Reilly at a tournament in Cincinnati in 2007. There was one towering difference; in those days, Reilly barely came up to Federer's shoulders. Now that he stands at 6ft 10in, it's the other way round.

CHAMPIONSHIPS **Day 13** NOTEBOOK

SUNDAY NIGHT FEVER

Just as Wimbledon itself seems to become more splendid by the year, so too, it seems, does its end-of-Championships celebration. The Champions' Dinner found a grand new venue at the Guildhall, the ceremonial and administrative centre of the City of London, a suitably lavish setting, not just for the tradition of the champions' dance to be revived, but also for beaming coach Boris Becker to welcome his charge Novak Djokovic to the three-time Wimbledon champions' club. Serena Williams, meanwhile, marked her reunion with the Venus Rosewater Dish with several selfies. It was a night to remember.

WIMBLEDON 2015

The Gentlemen's Singles

 Novak DJOKOVIC

The Ladies' Singles

 Serena WILLIAMS

The Gentlemen's Doubles

 Jean-Julien ROJER   **Horia TECAU**

The Ladies' Doubles

 Martina HINGIS   **Sania MIRZA**

The Mixed Doubles

 Leander PAES   **Martina HINGIS**

THE CHAMPIONS

The Boys' Singles

Reilly OPELKA

The Girls' Singles

Sofya ZHUK

The Boys' Doubles

**Nam Hoang LY
Sumit NAGAL**

The Girls' Doubles

**Dalma GALFI
Fanni STOLLAR**

The Gentlemen's Invitation Doubles

**Goran IVANISEVIC
Ivan LJUBICIC**

The Ladies' Invitation Doubles

**Magdalena MALEEVA
Rennae STUBBS**

The Gentlemen's Senior Invitation Doubles

**Jacco ELTINGH
Paul HAARHUIS**

The Gentlemen's Wheelchair Doubles

**Gustavo FERNANDEZ
Nicolas PEIFER**

The Ladies' Wheelchair Doubles

**Yui KAMIJI
Jordanne WHILEY**

EVENT I – THE GENTLEMEN'S SINGLES CHAMPIONSHIP 2015

Holder: NOVAK DJOKOVIC (SER)

The Champion will become the holder, for the year only, of the CHALLENGE CUP presented by The All England Lawn Tennis and Croquet Club in 1887. The Champion will receive a silver three-quarter size replica of the Challenge Cup. A Silver Salver will be presented to the Runner up and a Bronze Medal to each defeated semi-finalist. The matches will be the best of five sets.

First Round

1. **Novak Djokovic [1]** *(1)*....(SRB)
2. Philipp Kohlschreiber *(33)*....(GER)
3. Jarkko Nieminen *(92)*....(FIN)
4. (WC) Lleyton Hewitt *(118)*....(AUS)
5. (Q) Pierre-Hugues Herbert *(151)*....(FRA)
6. Hyeon Chung *(79)*....(KOR)
7. Jan-Lennard Struff *(112)*....(GER)
8. **Bernard Tomic [27]** *(26)*....(AUS)
9. **Leonardo Mayer [24]** *(21)*....(ARG)
10. Thanasi Kokkinakis *(71)*....(AUS)
11. Janko Tipsarevic *(39)*....(SRB)
12. Marcel Granollers *(72)*....(ESP)
13. Marsel Ilhan *(82)*....(TUR)
14. Jerzy Janowicz *(47)*....(POL)
15. Lucas Pouille *(96)*....(FRA)
16. **Kevin Anderson [14]** *(14)*....(RSA)
17. **Marin Cilic [9]** *(9)*....(CRO)
18. (Q) Hiroki Moriya *(174)*....(JPN)
19. Andreas Haider-Maurer *(57)*....(AUT)
20. Ricardas Berankis *(90)*....(LTU)
21. (WC) Matthew Ebden *(148)*....(AUS)
22. Blaz Rola *(93)*....(SLO)
23. Go Soeda *(91)*....(JPN)
24. **John Isner [17]** *(17)*....(USA)
25. **Pablo Cuevas [28]** *(23)*....(URU)
26. (WC) Denis Kudla *(105)*....(USA)
27. Teymuraz Gabashvili *(53)*....(RUS)
28. Alexander Zverev *(74)*....(GER)
29. Joao Souza *(81)*....(BRA)
30. Santiago Giraldo *(60)*....(COL)
31. Simone Bolelli *(55)*....(ITA)
32. **Kei Nishikori [5]** *(5)*....(JPN)
33. **Stan Wawrinka [4]** *(4)*....(SUI)
34. Joao Sousa *(46)*....(POR)
35. Victor Estrella Burgos *(48)*....(DOM)
36. Benjamin Becker *(51)*....(GER)
37. Martin Klizan *(39)*....(SVK)
38. Fernando Verdasco *(43)*....(ESP)
39. Dudi Sela *(85)*....(ISR)
40. **Dominic Thiem [32]** *(30)*....(AUT)
41. **Tommy Robredo [19]** *(19)*....(ESP)
42. (Q) John Millman *(120)*....(AUS)
43. Donald Young *(58)*....(USA)
44. Marcos Baghdatis *(54)*....(CYP)
45. (WC) Liam Broady *(182)*....(GBR)
46. Marinko Matosevic *(138)*....(AUS)
47. (Q) Horacio Zeballos *(128)*....(ARG)
48. **David Goffin [16]** *(15)*....(BEL)
49. **Grigor Dimitrov [11]** *(11)*....(BUL)
50. Federico Delbonis *(73)*....(ARG)
51. Lukas Lacko *(94)*....(SVK)
52. Steve Johnson *(52)*....(USA)
53. (Q) Kenny De Schepper *(163)*....(FRA)
54. (Q) John-Patrick Smith *(160)*....(AUS)
55. (Q) Luke Saville *(183)*....(AUS)
56. **Richard Gasquet [21]** *(20)*....(FRA)
57. **Nick Kyrgios [26]** *(29)*....(AUS)
58. Diego Schwartzman *(64)*....(ARG)
59. Juan Monaco *(35)*....(ARG)
60. Florian Mayer *(34)*....(GER)
61. Dusan Lajovic *(86)*....(SRB)
62. Tommy Haas *(25)*....(GER)
63. Daniel Gimeno-Traver *(63)*....(ESP)
64. **Milos Raonic [7]** *(8)*....(CAN)
65. (LL) Luca Vanni *(113)*....(ITA)
66. (WC) James Ward *(111)*....(GBR)
67. Jiri Vesely *(45)*....(CZE)
68. Paolo Lorenzi *(89)*....(ITA)
69. Vasek Pospisil *(56)*....(CAN)
70. (Q) Vincent Millot *(213)*....(FRA)
71. Tim Smyczek *(77)*....(USA)
72. **Fabio Fognini [30]** *(28)*....(ITA)
73. **Viktor Troicki [22]** *(24)*....(SRB)
74. (Q) Aleksandr Nedovyesov *(123)*....(KAZ)
75. Radek Stepanek *(57)*....(CZE)
76. Aljaz Bedene *(75)*....(GBR)
77. (Q) Dustin Brown *(102)*....(GER)
78. Yen-Hsun Lu *(61)*....(TPE)
79. Thomaz Bellucci *(42)*....(BRA)
80. **Rafael Nadal [10]** *(10)*....(ESP)
81. **Jo-Wilfried Tsonga [13]** *(12)*....(FRA)
82. Gilles Muller *(44)*....(LUX)
83. Denis Istomin *(62)*....(UZB)
84. Albert Ramos-Vinolas *(65)*....(ESP)
85. Alexandr Dolgopolov *(70)*....(UKR)
86. (WC) Kyle Edmund *(101)*....(GBR)
87. (Q) Elias Ymer *(133)*....(SWE)
88. **Ivo Karlovic [23]** *(25)*....(CRO)
89. **Andreas Seppi [25]** *(27)*....(ITA)
90. (WC) Brydan Klein *(177)*....(GBR)
91. Sergiy Stakhovsky *(49)*....(UKR)
92. Borna Coric *(40)*....(CRO)
93. Robin Haase *(78)*....(NED)
94. (Q) Alejandro Falla *(130)*....(COL)
95. Mikhail Kukushkin *(59)*....(KAZ)
96. **Andy Murray [3]** *(3)*....(GBR)
97. **Tomas Berdych [6]** *(6)*....(CZE)
98. Jeremy Chardy *(38)*....(FRA)
99. Filip Krajinovic *(122)*....(SRB)
100. (WC) Nicolas Mahut *(66)*....(FRA)
101. Ernests Gulbis *(83)*....(LAT)
102. Lukas Rosol *(41)*....(CZE)
103. Pablo Andujar *(37)*....(ESP)
104. **Guillermo Garcia-Lopez [29]** *(32)*....(ESP)
105. **Gael Monfils [18]** *(18)*....(FRA)
106. Pablo Carreno Busta *(67)*....(ESP)
107. Adrian Mannarino *(34)*....(FRA)
108. (Q) Michael Berrer *(139)*....(GER)
109. (Q) Yuichi Sugita *(149)*....(JPN)
110. Blaz Kavcic *(107)*....(SLO)
111. Nicolas Almagro *(27)*....(ESP)
112. **Gilles Simon [12]** *(13)*....(FRA)
113. **Feliciano Lopez [15]** *(16)*....(ESP)
114. Steve Darcis *(80)*....(BEL)
115. (Q) Nikoloz Basilashvili *(153)*....(GEO)
116. Facundo Bagnis *(137)*....(ARG)
117. Benoit Paire *(68)*....(FRA)
118. Mikhail Youzhny *(76)*....(RUS)
119. Ruben Bemelmans *(95)*....(BEL)
120. **Roberto Bautista Agut [20]** *(22)*....(ESP)
121. **Jack Sock [31]** *(31)*....(USA)
122. Sam Groth *(69)*....(AUS)
123. Malek Jaziri *(84)*....(TUN)
124. James Duckworth *(87)*....(AUS)
125. Sam Querrey *(36)*....(USA)
126. (Q) Igor Sijsling *(170)*....(NED)
127. Damir Dzumhur *(88)*....(BIH)
128. **Roger Federer [2]** *(2)*....(SUI)

Second Round

- **Novak Djokovic [1]**....6/4 6/4 6/4
- Jarkko Nieminen....3/6 6/3 4/6 6/0 11/9
- Pierre-Hugues Herbert..1/6 6/2 3/6 6/2 10/8
- **Bernard Tomic [27]**...6/3 3/6 2/6 6/2 6/3
- **Leonardo Mayer [24]**....7/6(7) 7/6(3) 6/4
- Marcel Granollers....6/3 6/4 6/2
- Marsel Ilhan....7/6(4) 6/4 6/7(4) 6/3
- **Kevin Anderson [14]**....6/2 7/5 3/6 6/3
- **Marin Cilic [9]**....6/3 6/2 7/6(4)
- Ricardas Berankis....6/2 5/2 Ret'd
- Matthew Ebden....6/2 6/1 6/4
- **John Isner [17]**....7/6(5) 6/4 6/4
- Denis Kudla....6/7(4) 4/6 6/3 6/2 6/2
- Alexander Zverev....6/3 1/6 6/3 3/6 9/7
- Santiago Giraldo....6/4 6/3 6/2
- **Kei Nishikori [5]**...6/3 6/7(4) 6/2 3/6 6/3
- **Stan Wawrinka [4]**....6/2 7/5 7/6(3)
- Victor Estrella Burgos....5/7 6/1 6/4 6/4
- Fernando Verdasco..4/6 6/2 6/3 6/7(5) 13/11
- **Dominic Thiem [32]**....2/6 6/3 6/4 6/4
- John Millman....6/2 6/3 6/4
- Marcos Baghdatis....5/7 6/2 6/4 6/4
- Liam Broady....5/7 4/6 6/3 6/2 6/3
- **David Goffin [16]**....7/6(4) 6/1 6/1
- **Grigor Dimitrov [11]**....6/3 6/0 6/4
- Steve Johnson....6/3 6/7(5) 4/6 6/1 6/4
- Kenny De Schepper..4/6 4/6 7/6(4) 6/4 6/4
- **Richard Gasquet [21]**....6/3 6/2 6/2
- **Nick Kyrgios [26]**....6/0 6/2 7/6(6)
- Juan Monaco....6/1 6/2 6/4
- Tommy Haas....6/2 6/3 4/6 6/2
- **Milos Raonic [7]**....6/2 6/3 3/6 7/6(4)
- James Ward....6/7(4) 6/2 6/4 6/3
- Jiri Vesely....7/6(7) 7/6(6) 6/4
- Vasek Pospisil..7/6(2) 3/6 6/7(4) 7/6(4) 6/3
- **Fabio Fognini [30]**....6/4 6/3 6/2
- **Viktor Troicki [22]**....6/1 6/4 3/6 6/3
- Aljaz Bedene....7/5 1/6 4/6 6/3 6/4
- Dustin Brown....3/6 6/3 7/5 6/4
- **Rafael Nadal [10]**....6/4 6/2 6/4
- **Jo-Wilfried Tsonga [13]**..7/6(8) 6/7(3) 6/4 3/6 6/2
- Albert Ramos-Vinolas....6/2 6/2 3/2 Ret'd
- Alexandr Dolgopolov....7/6(4) 6/1 6/2
- **Ivo Karlovic [23]**....6/7(2) 6/2 6/4 7/6(2)
- **Andreas Seppi [25]**....6/3 6/2 6/2
- Borna Coric....4/6 7/6(5) 6/2 1/6 9/7
- Robin Haase....6/2 3/6 6/4 6/2
- **Andy Murray [3]**....6/4 7/6(3) 6/4
- **Tomas Berdych [6]**..6/2 6/7(8) 7/6(3) 7/6(5)
- Nicolas Mahut....7/6(4) 6/4 3/6 7/5
- Lukas Rosol....7/6(2) 6/3 7/6(4)
- Pablo Andujar....3/6 6/4 3/6 7/5 6/4
- **Gael Monfils [18]**....6/4 6/4 7/5
- Adrian Mannarino....6/7(4) 6/0 6/4 6/1
- Blaz Kavcic....7/6(3) 6/3 7/6(5)
- **Gilles Simon [12]**....6/4 6/4 7/5
- **Feliciano Lopez [15]**....6/2 7/6(4) 6/4
- Nikoloz Basilashvili....6/4 7/6(3) 6/2
- Benoit Paire....6/4 6/4 6/3
- **Roberto Bautista Agut [20]**...6/1 6/3 7/6(6)
- Samuel Groth....6/3 3/6 6/3 6/3
- James Duckworth..7/6(2) 6/2 3/6 3/6 7/5
- Sam Querrey....7/5 6/3 6/4
- **Roger Federer [2]**....6/1 6/3 6/3

Third Round

- Novak Djokovic [1]....6/4 6/2 6/3
- Bernard Tomic [27]....7/6(3) 6/4 7/6(5)
- Leonardo Mayer [24]....6/3 7/6(4) 6/3
- Kevin Anderson [14]....6/7(5) 7/6(6) 6/4 6/4
- Marin Cilic [9]....6/3 4/6 7/6(6) 4/6 7/5
- John Isner [17]....6/2 7/6(8) 6/4
- Denis Kudla....6/3 3/6 7/6(2) 6/4
- Santiago Giraldo....w/o
- Stan Wawrinka [4]....6/3 6/4 7/5
- Fernando Verdasco....5/7 6/4 5/7 6/3 6/4
- Marcos Baghdatis....6/7(5) 2/6 6/3 6/2 6/4
- David Goffin [16]....7/6(3) 6/1 6/1
- Grigor Dimitrov [11]....7/6(8) 6/2 7/6(2)
- Richard Gasquet [21]....6/0 6/3 6/3
- Nick Kyrgios [26]....7/6(5) 6/3 6/4
- Milos Raonic [7]....6/0 6/2 6/7(5) 7/6(4)
- James Ward....6/2 7/6(4) 3/6 6/3
- Vasek Pospisil....6/3 6/4 1/6 6/3
- Viktor Troicki [22]....6/4 3/6 6/2 6/4
- Dustin Brown....7/5 3/6 6/4 6/4
- Jo-Wilfried Tsonga [13]....6/3 6/4 6/4
- Ivo Karlovic [23]....5/7 6/3 6/4 6/7(4) 13/11
- Andreas Seppi [25]....4/6 6/4 6/7(3) 6/1 6/1
- Andy Murray [3]....6/1 6/1 6/4
- Tomas Berdych [6]....6/1 6/4 6/4
- Pablo Andujar....6/4 1/6 4/6 7/6(4) 6/4
- Gael Monfils [18]....7/6(5) 6/3 7/5
- Gilles Simon [12]....6/1 6/1 6/7(5) 6/1
- Nikoloz Basilashvili....7/5 3/6 6/3 2/6 6/4
- Roberto Bautista Agut [20]....2/6 4/6 6/3 6/3 6/3
- Samuel Groth....7/5 6/4 7/6(6)
- Roger Federer [2]....6/4 6/2 6/2

Fourth Round

- Novak Djokovic [1]....6/3 6/3 6/3
- Kevin Anderson [14]....6/4 7/6(6) 6/3
- Marin Cilic [9]....7/6(4) 6/7(6) 6/4 6/7(4) 12/10
- Denis Kudla....6/2 6/7(3) 2/6 6/1 6/3
- Stan Wawrinka [4]....6/4 6/3 6/4
- David Goffin [16]....6/3 6/4 6/2
- Richard Gasquet [21]....6/3 6/4 6/4
- Nick Kyrgios [26]....5/7 7/5 7/6(3) 6/3
- Vasek Pospisil....6/4 3/6 2/6 6/3 8/6
- Viktor Troicki [22]....6/4 7/6(3) 4/6 6/3
- Ivo Karlovic [23]....7/6(3) 4/6 7/6(2) 7/6(9)
- Andy Murray [3]....6/2 6/2 1/6 6/1
- Tomas Berdych [6]....4/6 6/0 6/3 7/6(3)
- Gilles Simon [12]....3/6 6/3 7/6(6) 2/6 6/2
- Roberto Bautista Agut [20]....7/6(4) 6/0 6/1
- Roger Federer [2]....6/4 6/4 6/7(5) 6/2

Quarter-Finals

- Novak Djokovic [1]....6/7(6) 6/7(6) 6/1 6/4 7/5
- Marin Cilic [9]....6/4 4/6 6/3 7/5
- Stan Wawrinka [4]....7/6(3) 7/6(7) 6/4
- Richard Gasquet [21]....7/5 6/1 6/7(7) 7/6(6)
- Vasek Pospisil....4/6 6/7(4) 6/4 6/3 6/3
- Andy Murray [3]....7/6(7) 6/4 5/7 6/4
- Gilles Simon [12]....6/3 6/3 6/2
- Roger Federer [2]....6/2 6/2 6/3

Semi-Finals

- Novak Djokovic [1] 6/4 6/4 6/4
- Richard Gasquet [21] 6/4 4/6 3/6 6/4 11/9
- Andy Murray [3] 6/4 7/5 6/4
- Roger Federer [2] 6/3 7/5 6/2

Final

- Novak Djokovic [1] 7/6(2) 6/4 6/4
- Roger Federer [2] 7/5 7/5 6/4

Champion

Novak Djokovic [1] 7/6(1) 6/7(10) 6/4 6/3

Heavy type denotes seeded players. The figure in brackets against names denotes the order in which they have been seeded. The figures in italics denotes ATP World Tour Ranking -29.06.2015
(WC)=Wild card. (Q)=Qualifier. (LL)=Lucky loser.

EVENT II – THE GENTLEMEN'S DOUBLES CHAMPIONSHIP 2015
Holders: VASEK POSPISIL (CAN) & JACK SOCK (USA)

The Champions will become the holders, for the year only, of the CHALLENGE CUPS presented by the OXFORD UNIVERSITY LAWN TENNIS CLUB in 1884 and the late SIR HERBERT WILBERFORCE in 1937.
The Champions will receive a silver three-quarter size replica of the Challenge Cup. A Silver Salver will be presented to each of the Runners-up, and a Bronze Medal to each defeated semi-finalist. The matches will be the best of five sets.

First Round · Second Round · Third Round · Quarter-Finals · Semi-Finals · Final

1. Bob Bryan (USA) & Mike Bryan (USA) ....[1]
(LL) 2. Gero Kretschmer (GER) & Alexander Satschko (GER)..
Bob Bryan & Mike Bryan [1] 6/3 6/4 6/3
3. Steve Johnson (USA) & Sam Querrey (USA)............
4. Aljaz Bedene (GBR) & Damir Dzumhur (BIH).............
Steve Johnson & Sam Querrey 6/1 6/3 6/3
Bob Bryan & Mike Bryan [1] ......6/1 5/7 7/6(3) 6/3
5. Santiago Giraldo (COL) & Joao Sousa (POR) ....
6. Mate Pavic (CRO) & Michael Venus (NZL)................
Mate Pavic & Michael Venus 4/6 6/3 6/4 6/2
Bob Bryan & Mike Bryan [1] ......7/6(4) 6/3 6/1
7. Pablo Andujar (ESP) & Oliver Marach (AUT) ....
8. Raven Klaasen (RSA) & Rajeev Ram (USA)........[14]
Raven Klaasen & Rajeev Ram [14] ......7/6(2) 6/4 2/6 6/7(5) 8/6
Mate Pavic & Michael Venus ......7/6(4) 6/4 3/6 6/7(5) 11/9
9. Rohan Bopanna (IND) & Florin Mergea (ROU)..[9]
10. Tim Smyczek (USA) & Jiri Vesely (CZE)....................
Rohan Bopanna & Florin Mergea [9] ......6/3 7/6(1) 6/1
Rohan Bopanna & Florin Mergea [9]
11. Radek Stepanek (CZE) & Mikhail Youzhny (RUS)......
12. Thomaz Bellucci (BRA) & Guillermo Duran (ARG)...
Thomaz Bellucci & Guillermo Duran ......5/7 6/4 6/2 6/7(5) 6/3
Rohan Bopanna & Florin Mergea [9] ......7/5 7/6(5) 7/6(5)
13. Adrian Mannarino (FRA) & Lucas Pouille (FRA) ....
14. Lukasz Kubot (POL) & Max Mirnyi (BLR) ....
Lukasz Kubot & Max Mirnyi 7/5 6/4 6/3
Rohan Bopanna & Florin Mergea [9] ...7/6(4) 6/7(5) 7/6(5) 7/6(8)
15. Mateusz Kowalczyk (POL) & Igor Zelenay (SVK) .....
(Q) 16. Marcel Granollers (ESP) & Marc Lopez (ESP) .....[6]
Marcel Granollers & Marc Lopez [6] ......3/6 4/6 7/6(6) 6/4 15/13
Lukasz Kubot & Max Mirnyi 6/4 6/3 6/4
17. Jean-Julien Rojer (NED) & Horia Tecau (ROU)..[4]
18. Martin Klizan (SVK) & Lukas Rosol (CZE) ....
Jean-Julien Rojer & Horia Tecau [4] ......3/0 Ret'd
Jean-Julien Rojer & Horia Tecau [4]
19. Victor Estrella Burgos (DOM) & Joao Souza (BRA)
20. Andre Begemann (GER) & Julian Knowle (AUT) .....
Andre Begemann & Julian Knowle ......6/4 7/6(3) 3/6 7/5
Jean-Julien Rojer & Horia Tecau [4] 1/6 3/6 6/4 6/2 15/13
21. Robert Lindstedt (SWE) & Jurgen Melzer (AUT).......
22. Mahesh Bhupathi (IND) & Janko Tipsarevic (SRB)...
Robert Lindstedt & Jurgen Melzer 6/3 6/3 6/2
Lleyton Hewitt & Thanasi Kokkinakis ......6/3 3/6 4/6 7/6(6) 6/4
(WC) 23. Lleyton Hewitt (AUS) & Thanasi Kokkinakis (AUS)..
24. Marin Draganja (CRO) & Henri Kontinen (FIN)..[15]
Lleyton Hewitt & Thanasi Kokkinakis ......6/7(6) 3/6 7/6(1) 6/2 8/6
Jean-Julien Rojer & Horia Tecau [4] ......7/6(7) 6/3 7/6(1)
25. Pierre-Hugues Herbert (FRA) & Nicolas Mahut (FRA)..[10]
26. Nicolas Almagro (ESP) & Adrian Menendez-Maceiras (ESP)..
Pierre-Hugues Herbert & Nicolas Mahut [10] ......1/6 7/6(3) 6/3 4/6 6/3
Pierre-Hugues Herbert & Nicolas Mahut [10]
27. Gilles Muller (LUX) & Aisam Qureshi (PAK)..............
28. Benjamin Becker (GER) & Roberto Maytin (VEN)......
Gilles Muller & Aisam Qureshi 6/3 6/3 6/3
Pierre-Hugues Herbert & Nicolas Mahut [10] ......6/7(9) 7/6(4) 6/4 6/4
29. Dominic Inglot (GBR) & Edouard Roger-Vasselin (FRA) ..
30. Rameez Junaid (AUS) & Adil Shamasdin (CAN) ....
Dominic Inglot & Edouard Roger-Vasselin ......7/6(4) 3/6 6/7(4) 6/2
Marcin Matkowski & Nenad Zimonjic [7] ......6/7(4) 2/6 7/6(3) 6/4 6/3
(WC) 31. Ken Skupski (GBR) & Neal Skupski (GBR)..................
32. Marcin Matkowski (POL) & Nenad Zimonjic (SRB)..[7]
Marcin Matkowski & Nenad Zimonjic [7] ......7/6(5) 1/6 4/6 7/6(4) 6/4
Marcin Matkowski & Nenad Zimonjic [7] ......7/6(7) 3/6 7/5 6/1
33. Alexander Peya (AUT) & Bruno Soares (BRA)....[8]
34. Pablo Carreno Busta (ESP) & Daniel Gimeno-Traver (ESP)...
Alexander Peya & Bruno Soares [8] ......6/3 6/4 6/7(5) 6/1
Alexander Peya & Bruno Soares [8]
(Q) 35. Sergey Betov (BLR) & Alexander Bury (BLR) ....
(WC) 36. Edward Corrie (GBR) & Kyle Edmund (GBR) ....
Sergey Betov & Alexander Bury 7/5 6/4 6/3
Alexander Peya & Bruno Soares [8] ......6/1 7/6(6) 4/6 6/1
(WC) 37. Matthew Ebden (AUS) & James Ward (GBR) ....
38. Teymuraz Gabashvili (RUS) & Yen-Hsun Lu (TPE)...
Teymuraz Gabashvili & Yen-Hsun Lu ......7/5 6/2 7/6(3)
Daniel Nestor & Leander Paes [11] ......5/7 7/6(3) 7/6(4) 7/5
39. Dusan Lajovic (SRB) & Viktor Troicki (SRB) ....
40. Daniel Nestor (CAN) & Leander Paes (IND) ....[11]
Daniel Nestor & Leander Paes [11] 6/3 6/4 7/5
Alexander Peya & Bruno Soares [8] 6/3 7/5 3/6 2/6 6/2
41. Jamie Murray (GBR) & John Peers (AUS).............[13]
(WC) 42. Luke Bambridge (GBR) & Liam Broady (GBR) ....
Jamie Murray & John Peers [13] ......6/1 7/6(2) 6/2
Jamie Murray & John Peers [13]
43. Nicholas Monroe (USA) & Artem Sitak (NZL)............
44. Dustin Brown (GER) & Andreas Haider-Maurer (AUT)..
Nicholas Monroe & Artem Sitak ......7/6(3) 4/6 6/4 3/6 10/8
Jamie Murray & John Peers [13] ......7/5 4/6 4/6 7/6(5) 6/4
45. Eric Butorac (USA) & Colin Fleming (GBR)..............
46. Frantisek Cermak (CZE) & Philipp Oswald (AUT) ....
Eric Butorac & Colin Fleming ......6/7(5) 7/5 7/5 3/2 Ret'd
Vasek Pospisil & Jack Sock [3] ......6/3 6/3 7/6(4)
47. Samuel Groth (AUS) & Sergiy Stakhovsky (UKR) .....
48. Vasek Pospisil (CAN) & Jack Sock (USA) ....[3]
Vasek Pospisil & Jack Sock [3] ......5/7 7/6(5) 7/6(3) 6/1
Jamie Murray & John Peers [13] ......6/3 7/6(6) 6/7(5) 3/6 8/6
49. Simone Bolelli (ITA) & Fabio Fognini (ITA)..........[5]
50. Guillermo Garcia-Lopez (ESP) & Malek Jaziri (TUN)..
Guillermo Garcia-Lopez & Malek Jaziri ......7/5 7/6(2) 6/3
Marcus Daniell & Marcelo Demoliner
(LL) 51. Marcus Daniell (NZL) & Marcelo Demoliner (BRA)..
52. Robin Haase (NED) & Benoit Paire (FRA)..............
Marcus Daniell & Marcelo Demoliner ......6/3 7/6(4) 6/1
Marcus Daniell & Marcelo Demoliner ......w/o
53. Albert Ramos-Vinolas (ESP) & Andreas Seppi (ITA)....
(Q) 54. Jonathan Erlich (ISR) & Philipp Petzschner (GER)...
Jonathan Erlich & Philipp Petzschner 6/4 6/2 4/6 6/3
Jonathan Erlich & Philipp Petzschner
55. Treat Huey (PHI) & Scott Lipsky (USA)....................
56. Pablo Cuevas (URU) & David Marrero (ESP)......[12]
Treat Huey & Scott Lipsky ......7/6(2) 6/2 6/4
Jonathan Erlich & Philipp Petzschner ......6/3 7/5 7/6(3)
57. Juan-Sebastian Cabal (COL) & Robert Farah (COL)..[16]
58. Chris Guccione (AUS) & Andre Sa (BRA)................
Juan-Sebastian Cabal & Robert Farah [16] ......6/4 3/6 4/6 7/6(2) 6/3
Jonathan Marray & Frederik Nielsen
(WC) 59. Jonathan Marray (GBR) & Frederik Nielsen (DEN)...
(Q) 60. Fabrice Martin (FRA) & Purav Raja (IND).................
Jonathan Marray & Frederik Nielsen ......6/1 6/4 4/6 7/6(7)
Jonathan Marray & Frederik Nielsen 6/3 5/7 7/5 6/4
61. Radu Albot (MDA) & Mikhail Kukushkin (KAZ).........
62. Mariusz Fyrstenberg (POL) & Santiago Gonzalez (MEX)..
Mariusz Fyrstenberg & Santiago Gonzalez 6/4 6/3 6/4
Ivan Dodig & Marcelo Melo [2]
63. Leonardo Mayer (ARG) & Diego Sebastian Schwartzman (ARG)..
64. Ivan Dodig (CRO) & Marcelo Melo (BRA) ....[2]
Ivan Dodig & Marcelo Melo [2] ......6/4 4/0 Ret'd
Ivan Dodig & Marcelo Melo [2] ...7/6(2) 6/7(4) 2/6 7/6(5) 6/4

Bob Bryan & Mike Bryan [1]

Rohan Bopanna & Florin Mergea [9] ...5/7 6/4 7/6(9) 7/6(5)

Rohan Bopanna & Florin Mergea [9]

Jean-Julien Rojer & Horia Tecau [4] ...4/6 6/2 6/3 4/6 13/11

Jean-Julien Rojer & Horia Tecau [4] ...6/4 6/3 7/6(2)

Jean-Julien Rojer & Horia Tecau [4] ...7/6(5) 6/4 6/4

Marcin Matkowski & Nenad Zimonjic [7]

Alexander Peya & Bruno Soares [8]

Jamie Murray & John Peers [13] ...6/4 7/6(3) 6/3

Jamie Murray & John Peers [13]

Jonathan Erlich & Philipp Petzschner ...4/6 6/2 6/2 6/4

Ivan Dodig & Marcelo Melo [2] ...6/1 6/4 7/6(6)

Jamie Murray & John Peers [13] ...4/6 6/3 6/4 6/2

Heavy type denotes seeded players. The figure in brackets against names denotes the order in which they have been seeded.
(WC)=Wild card. (Q)=Qualifier. (LL)=Lucky loser.

EVENT III – THE LADIES' SINGLES CHAMPIONSHIP 2015

Holder: PETRA KVITOVA (CZE)

The Champion will become the holder, for the year only, of the CHALLENGE TROPHY presented by The All England Lawn Tennis and Croquet Club in 1886. The Champion will receive a silver three-quarter size replica of the Challenge Trophy. A Silver Salver will be presented to the Runner up and a Bronze Medal to each defeated semi-finalist. The matches will be the best of three sets.

First Round

1. **Serena Williams [1]** *(1)* (USA)
2. (Q) Margarita Gasparyan *(113)* (RUS)
3. Timea Babos *(93)* (HUN)
4. (Q) Petra Cetkovska *(162)* (CZE)
5. Daniela Hantuchova *(72)* (SVK)
6. Dominika Cibulkova *(45)* (SVK)
7. Heather Watson *(59)* (GBR)
8. **Caroline Garcia [32]** *(33)* (FRA)
9. **Sara Errani [19]** *(19)* (ITA)
10. Francesca Schiavone *(80)* (ITA)
11. Aleksandra Krunic *(82)* (SRB)
12. Roberta Vinci *(35)* (ITA)
13. Marina Erakovic *(86)* (NZL)
14. Yulia Putintseva *(95)* (KAZ)
15. Madison Brengle *(36)* (USA)
16. **Venus Williams [16]** *(16)* (USA)
17. **Carla Suárez Navarro [9]** *(9)* (ESP)
18. (WC) Jelena Ostapenko *(147)* (LAT)
19. Alexandra Dulgheru *(60)* (ROU)
20. Kristina Mladenovic *(38)* (FRA)
21. Kirsten Flipkens *(96)* (BEL)
22. Annika Beck *(70)* (GER)
23. (WC) Anett Kontaveit *(145)* (EST)
24. **Victoria Azarenka [23]** *(24)* (BLR)
25. **Belinda Bencic [30]** *(22)* (SUI)
26. Tsvetana Pironkova *(41)* (BUL)
27. Vitalia Diatchenko *(74)* (RUS)
28. Anna-Lena Friedsam *(87)* (GER)
29. Alison Van Uytvanck *(46)* (BEL)
30. (Q) Bethanie Mattek-Sands *(158)* (USA)
31. (Q) Yi-Fan Xu *(176)* (CHN)
32. **Ana Ivanovic [7]** *(7)* (SRB)
33. **Maria Sharapova [4]** *(4)* (RUS)
34. (WC) Johanna Konta *(126)* (GBR)
35. (Q) Richel Hogenkamp *(123)* (NED)
36. Qiang Wang *(110)* (CHN)
37. Nicole Gibbs *(103)* (USA)
38. Lesia Tsurenko *(68)* (UKR)
39. Daria Gavrilova *(39)* (AUS)
40. **Irina-Camelia Begu [29]** *(31)* (ROU)
41. **Flavia Pennetta [24]** *(26)* (ITA)
42. Zarina Diyas *(34)* (KAZ)
43. Lin Zhu *(116)* (CHN)
44. (Q) Aliaksandra Sasnovich *(137)* (BLR)
45. Mariana Duque-Mariño *(99)* (COL)
46. (WC) Naomi Broady *(200)* (GBR)
47. Shelby Rogers *(84)* (USA)
48. **Andrea Petkovic [14]** *(14)* (GER)
49. **Karolina Pliskova [11]** *(11)* (CZE)
50. Irina Falconi *(69)* (USA)
51. Coco Vandeweghe *(47)* (USA)
52. Anna Karolina Schmiedlova *(63)* (SVK)
53. Edina Gallovits-Hall *(109)* (USA)
54. Urszula Radwanska *(107)* (POL)
55. Danka Kovinic *(92)* (MNE)
56. **Samantha Stosur [22]** *(23)* (AUS)
57. **Barbora Strycova [27]** *(29)* (CZE)
58. Sloane Stephens *(37)* (USA)
59. Polona Hercog *(76)* (SLO)
60. Lauren Davis *(75)* (USA)
61. (Q) Su-Wei Hsieh *(131)* (TPE)
62. Kaia Kanepi *(50)* (EST)
63. Alison Riske *(44)* (USA)
64. **Lucie Safarova [6]** *(6)* (CZE)
65. **Caroline Wozniacki [5]** *(5)* (DEN)
66. Saisai Zheng *(66)* (CHN)
67. Katerina Siniakova *(67)* (CZE)
68. Denisa Allertova *(83)* (CZE)
69. Lara Arruabarrena *(85)* (ESP)
70. Pauline Parmentier *(105)* (FRA)
71. Teliana Pereira *(77)* (BRA)
72. **Camila Giorgi [31]** *(32)* (ITA)
73. **Garbiñe Muguruza [20]** *(20)* (ESP)
74. Varvara Lepchenko *(40)* (USA)
75. Mirjana Lucic-Baroni *(54)* (CRO)
76. Yaroslava Shvedova *(79)* (KAZ)
77. Anastasia Pavlyuchenkova *(42)* (RUS)
78. Mona Barthel *(49)* (GER)
79. Carina Witthoeft *(53)* (GER)
80. **Angelique Kerber [10]** *(10)* (GER)
81. **Timea Bacsinszky [15]** *(15)* (SUI)
82. Julia Goerges *(56)* (GER)
83. Sesil Karatantcheva *(98)* (BUL)
84. Silvia Soler-Espinosa *(102)* (ESP)
85. Johanna Larsson *(73)* (SWE)
86. Christina McHale *(64)* (USA)
87. Jarmila Gajdosova *(58)* (AUS)
88. **Sabine Lisicki [18]** *(18)* (GER)
89. **Svetlana Kuznetsova [26]** *(25)* (RUS)
90. (Q) Laura Siegemund *(128)* (GER)
91. Kristyna Pliskova *(134)* (CZE)
92. Tereza Smitkova *(62)* (CZE)
93. Monica Puig *(91)* (PUR)
94. Monica Niculescu *(48)* (ROU)
95. Jana Cepelova *(106)* (SVK)
96. **Simona Halep [3]** *(3)* (ROU)
97. **Ekaterina Makarova [8]** *(8)* (RUS)
98. (Q) Sachia Vickery *(112)* (USA)
99. Karin Knapp *(43)* (ITA)
100. Magdalena Rybarikova *(65)* (SVK)
101. Andreea Mitu *(71)* (ROU)
102. (Q) Olga Govortsova *(122)* (BLR)
103. Ana Konjuh *(55)* (CRO)
104. **Alizé Cornet [25]** *(27)* (FRA)
105. **Madison Keys [21]** *(21)* (USA)
106. Stefanie Voegele *(104)* (SUI)
107. Yanina Wickmayer *(88)* (BEL)
108. Elizaveta Kulichkova *(109)* (RUS)
109. Tatjana Maria *(78)* (GER)
110. Bojana Jovanovski *(51)* (SRB)
111. (Q) Ying-Ying Duan *(117)* (CHN)
112. **Eugenie Bouchard [12]** *(12)* (CAN)
113. **Agnieszka Radwanska [13]** *(13)* (POL)
114. Lucie Hradecka *(52)* (CZE)
115. Ajla Tomljanovic *(81)* (AUS)
116. Klara Koukalova *(100)* (CZE)
117. (Q) Tamira Paszek *(243)* (AUT)
118. Casey Dellacqua *(61)* (AUS)
119. Misaki Doi *(94)* (JPN)
120. **Elina Svitolina [17]** *(17)* (UKR)
121. **Jelena Jankovic [28]** *(30)* (SRB)
122. Elena Vesnina *(89)* (RUS)
123. Evgeniya Rodina *(101)* (RUS)
124. (WC) Laura Robson (GBR)
125. Magda Linette *(97)* (POL)
126. Kurumi Nara *(57)* (JPN)
127. Kiki Bertens *(108)* (NED)
128. **Petra Kvitova [2]** *(2)* (CZE)

Second Round

- **Serena Williams [1]** 6/4 6/1
- Timea Babos 7/6(4) 6/3
- Daniela Hantuchova 7/5 6/0
- Heather Watson 1/6 6/3 8/6
- **Sara Errani [19]** 6/2 5/7 6/1
- Aleksandra Krunic 6/2 6/4
- Yulia Putintseva 7/6(5) 7/5
- **Venus Williams [16]** 6/0 6/0
- Jelena Ostapenko 6/2 6/0
- Kristina Mladenovic 6/2 6/1
- Kirsten Flipkens 0/6 6/3 6/4
- **Victoria Azarenka [23]** 6/2 6/1
- **Belinda Bencic [30]** 3/6 6/1 6/3
- Anna-Lena Friedsam 3/6 6/3 7/5
- Bethanie Mattek-Sands 6/3 6/2
- **Ana Ivanovic [7]** 6/1 6/1
- **Maria Sharapova [4]** 6/2 6/2
- Richel Hogenkamp 6/4 6/4
- Lesia Tsurenko 6/3 6/3
- **Irina-Camelia Begu [29]** 7/6(6) 6/1
- Zarina Diyas 6/3 2/6 6/4
- Aliaksandra Sasnovich 4/6 7/5 6/1
- Mariana Duque-Marino 7/6(5) 6/3
- **Andrea Petkovic [14]** 6/0 6/0
- **Karolina Pliskova [11]** 6/4 4/6 6/1
- Coco Vandeweghe 6/4 6/2
- Urszula Radwanska 6/2 6/1
- **Samantha Stosur [22]** 6/4 6/4
- Sloane Stephens 6/4 6/2
- Lauren Davis 6/4 7/6(3)
- Su-Wei Hsieh 6/1 6/4
- **Lucie Safarova [6]** 3/6 7/5 6/3
- **Caroline Wozniacki [5]** 7/5 6/0
- Denisa Allertova 6/2 4/6 6/3
- Lara Arruabarrena 6/4 6/2
- **Camila Giorgi [31]** 7/6(4) 6/3
- **Garbiñe Muguruza [20]** 6/4 6/1
- Mirjana Lucic-Baroni 7/5 6/7(5) 7/5
- Anastasia Pavlyuchenkova 6/7(3) 7/6(4) 6/2
- **Angelique Kerber [10]** 6/0 6/0
- **Timea Bacsinszky [15]** 6/2 7/5
- Silvia Soler-Espinosa 2/6 6/2 7/5
- Christina McHale 6/3 6/2
- **Sabine Lisicki [18]** 7/5 6/4
- **Svetlana Kuznetsova [26]** 6/3 6/4
- Kristyna Pliskova 3/6 7/5 7/5
- Monica Niculescu 5/7 6/3 6/1
- Jana Cepelova 5/7 6/4 6/3
- **Ekaterina Makarova [8]** 6/2 6/4
- Magdalena Rybarikova 7/6(6) 3/0 Ret'd
- Olga Govortsova 6/1 6/1
- **Alize Cornet [25]** 6/2 6/2
- **Madison Keys [21]** 6/7(6) 6/3 6/4
- Elizaveta Kulichkova 3/6 7/6(6) 10/8
- Tatjana Maria 7/6(2) 7/5
- Ying-Ying Duan 7/6(3) 6/4
- **Agnieszka Radwanska [13]** 6/3 6/2
- Ajla Tomljanovic 6/3 6/4
- Casey Dellacqua 6/2 6/2
- **Elina Svitolina [17]** 3/6 6/3 6/2
- **Jelena Jankovic [28]** 6/4 3/6 10/8
- Evgeniya Rodina 6/4 6/4
- Kurumi Nara 3/6 6/3 4/3 Ret'd
- **Petra Kvitova [2]** 6/1 6/0

Third Round

- **Serena Williams [1]** 6/4 6/1
- Heather Watson 6/4 6/2
- Aleksandra Krunic 6/3 6/7(2) 6/2
- **Venus Williams [16]** 7/6(5) 6/4
- Kristina Mladenovic 6/4 7/5
- **Victoria Azarenka [23]** 6/3 6/3
- **Belinda Bencic [30]** 7/5 4/6 6/0
- Bethanie Mattek-Sands 6/3 6/4
- **Maria Sharapova [4]** 6/3 6/1
- **Irina-Camelia Begu [29]** 7/5 6/7(4) 7/5
- Zarina Diyas 7/5 6/1
- **Andrea Petkovic [14]** 6/3 6/1
- Coco Vandeweghe 7/6(5) 6/4
- **Samantha Stosur [22]** 6/3 6/4
- Sloane Stephens 6/4 6/4
- **Lucie Safarova [6]** 6/2 6/3
- **Caroline Wozniacki [5]** 6/1 7/6(6)
- **Camila Giorgi [31]** 6/0 7/6(5)
- **Garbiñe Muguruza [20]** 6/3 4/6 6/2
- **Angelique Kerber [10]** 7/5 6/2
- **Timea Bacsinszky [15]** 6/2 6/1
- **Sabine Lisicki [18]** 2/6 7/5 6/1
- Kristyna Pliskova 3/6 6/3 6/4
- Monica Niculescu 6/3 6/3
- Magdalena Rybarikova 6/2 7/5
- Olga Govortsova 7/6(6) 2/6 6/1
- **Madison Keys [21]** 6/4 7/6(3)
- Tatjana Maria 1/6 6/2 10/8
- **Agnieszka Radwanska [13]** 6/0 6/2
- Casey Dellacqua 7/6(3) 6/3
- **Jelena Jankovic [28]** 6/7(4) 6/1 6/3
- **Petra Kvitova [2]** 6/2 6/0

Fourth Round

- **Serena Williams [1]** 6/2 4/6 7/5
- **Venus Williams [16]** 6/3 6/2
- **Victoria Azarenka [23]** 6/4 6/4
- **Belinda Bencic [30]** 7/5 7/5
- **Maria Sharapova [4]** 6/4 6/3
- Zarina Diyas 7/5 6/4
- Coco Vandeweghe 6/2 6/0
- **Lucie Safarova [6]** 3/6 6/3 6/1
- **Caroline Wozniacki [5]** 6/2 6/2
- **Garbiñe Muguruza [20]** 7/6(12) 1/6 6/2
- **Timea Bacsinszky [15]** 6/3 6/2
- Monica Niculescu 6/3 7/5
- Olga Govortsova 7/6(4) 6/3
- **Madison Keys [21]** 6/4 6/4
- **Agnieszka Radwanska [13]** 6/1 6/4
- **Jelena Jankovic [28]** 3/6 7/5 6/4

Quarter-Finals

- **Serena Williams [1]** 6/4 6/3
- **Victoria Azarenka [23]** 6/2 6/3
- **Maria Sharapova [4]** 6/4 6/4
- Coco Vandeweghe 7/6(1) 7/6(4)
- **Garbiñe Muguruza [20]** 6/4 6/4
- **Timea Bacsinszky [15]** 1/6 7/5 6/2
- **Madison Keys [21]** 3/6 6/4 6/1
- **Agnieszka Radwanska [13]** 7/5 6/4

Semi-Finals

- **Serena Williams [1]** 3/6 6/2 6/3
- **Maria Sharapova [4]** 6/3 6/7(3) 6/2
- **Garbiñe Muguruza [20]** 7/5 6/3
- **Agnieszka Radwanska [13]** 7/6(3) 3/6 6/3

Final

- **Serena Williams [1]** 6/2 6/4
- **Garbiñe Muguruza [20]** 6/2 3/6 6/3

Champion: Serena Williams [1] 6/4 6/4

Heavy type denotes seeded players. The figure in brackets against names denotes the order in which they have been seeded. The figures in italics denotes WTA Ranking – 29.06.2015

(WC)=Wild card. (Q)=Qualifier. (LL)=Lucky loser.

EVENT IV – THE LADIES' DOUBLES CHAMPIONSHIP 2015
Holders: SARA ERRANI (ITA) & ROBERTA VINCI (ITA)

The Champions will become the holders, for the year only, of the CHALLENGE CUPS presented by H.R.H. PRINCESS MARINA, DUCHESS OF KENT, the late President of The All England Lawn Tennis and Croquet Club in 1949 and The All England Lawn Tennis and Croquet Club in 2001.
The Champions will receive a silver three-quarter size replica of the Challenge Cup. A Silver Salver will be presented to each of the Runners-up and a Bronze Medal to each defeated semi-finalist. The matches will be the best of three sets.

First Round	Second Round	Third Round	Quarter-Finals	Semi-Finals	Final

1. **Martina Hingis** (SUI) & **Sania Mirza** (IND)......................**[1]**
2. Zarina Diyas (KAZ) & Saisai Zheng (CHN)

Martina Hingis & Sania Mirza [1]
6/2 6/2

3. Klaudia Jans-Ignacik (POL) & Andreja Klepac (SLO)
4. Kimiko Date-Krumm (JPN) & Francesca Schiavone (ITA)

Kimiko Date-Krumm & Francesca Schiavone
6/4 6/2

Martina Hingis & Sania Mirza [1]
6/0 6/1

5. Bojana Jovanovski (SRB) & Nadiia Kichenok (UKR)
6. Marina Erakovic (NZL) & Heather Watson (GBR)

Marina Erakovic & Heather Watson
6/4 7/6(4)

(Q) 7. Elizaveta Kulichkova (RUS) & Evgeniya Rodina (RUS)
8. **Anabel Medina Garrigues** (ESP) & **Arantxa Parra Santonja** (ESP)...**[16]**

Anabel Medina Garrigues & Arantxa Parra Santonja [16]
3/6 6/3 6/4

Anabel Medina Garrigues & Arantxa Parra Santonja [16]
7/6(2) 3/6 6/0

Martina Hingis & Sania Mirza [1]
6/4 6/3

9. **Casey Dellacqua** (AUS) & **Yaroslava Shvedova** (KAZ)...**[9]**
10. Gabriela Dabrowski (CAN) & Alicja Rosolska (POL)

Casey Dellacqua & Yaroslava Shvedova [9]
6/4 6/4

11. Daniela Hantuchova (SVK) & Samantha Stosur (AUS)
12. Janette Husarova (SVK) & Paula Kania (POL)

Daniela Hantuchova & Samantha Stosur
6/1 7/5

Casey Dellacqua & Yaroslava Shvedova [9]
6/3 6/0

13. Karin Knapp (ITA) & Roberta Vinci (ITA)
(LL) 14. Chin-Wei Chan (TPE) & Nicole Melichar (USA)

Karin Knapp & Roberta Vinci
6/2 6/4

Casey Dellacqua & Yaroslava Shvedova [9]
4/6 6/2 8/6

15. Alize Cornet (FRA) & Aleksandra Krunic (SRB)
16. **Andrea Hlavackova** (CZE) & **Lucie Hradecka** (CZE)...**[8]**

Andrea Hlavackova & Lucie Hradecka [8]
6/1 6/4

Karin Knapp & Roberta Vinci
6/3 3/6 6/4

Martina Hingis & Sania Mirza [1]
7/5 6/3

17. **Bethanie Mattek-Sands** (USA) & **Lucie Safarova** (CZE)...**[3]**
(WC) 18. Naomi Broady (GBR) & Emily Webley-Smith (GBR)

Bethanie Mattek-Sands & Lucie Safarova [3]
6/3 6/2

(LL) 19. Jana Cepelova (SVK) & Stefanie Voegele (SUI)
(WC) 20. Jocelyn Rae (GBR) & Anna Smith (GBR)

Jocelyn Rae & Anna Smith
6/2 6/1

Bethanie Mattek-Sands & Lucie Safarova [3]
6/3 6/0

21. Varvara Lepchenko (USA) & Christina McHale (USA)
22. Lara Arruabarrena (ESP) & Irina-Camelia Begu (ROU)

Lara Arruabarrena & Irina-Camelia Begu
6/4 6/4

23. Jarmila Gajdosova (AUS) & Ajla Tomljanovic (AUS)
24. **Yung-Jan Chan** (TPE) & **Jie Zheng** (CHN)................**[13]**

Jarmila Gajdosova & Ajla Tomljanovic
2/6 6/4 6/2

Jarmila Gajdosova & Ajla Tomljanovic
6/4 6/4

Bethanie Mattek-Sands & Lucie Safarova [3]
7/5 6/2

(LL) 25. Misaki Doi (JPN) & Stephanie Vogt (LIE)
(WC) 26. Johanna Konta (GBR) & Maria Sanchez (USA)

Johanna Konta & Maria Sanchez
6/3 7/6(5)

27. Julia Goerges (GER) & Carina Witthoeft (GER)
28. Hao-Ching Chan (TPE) & Alison Van Uytvanck (BEL)

Hao-Ching Chan & Alison Van Uytvanck
6/2 6/2

Hao-Ching Chan & Alison Van Uytvanck
7/6(5) 6/2

29. Darija Jurak (CRO) & Ana Konjuh (CRO)
30. Jelena Jankovic (SRB) & Mirjana Lucic-Baroni (CRO)

Darija Jurak & Ana Konjuh
6/3 6/3

Raquel Kops-Jones & Abigail Spears [5]
6/2 6/4

31. Kiki Bertens (NED) & Alison Riske (USA)
32. **Raquel Kops-Jones** (USA) & **Abigail Spears** (USA)...**[5]**

Raquel Kops-Jones & Abigail Spears [5]
6/3 6/2

Raquel Kops-Jones & Abigail Spears [5]
6/3 6/4

Raquel Kops-Jones & Abigail Spears [5]
6/3 6/2

Martina Hingis & Sania Mirza [1]
6/1 6/2

33. **Su-Wei Hsieh** (TPE) & **Flavia Pennetta** (ITA)..........**[7]**
34. Elena Bogdan (ROU) & Simona Halep (ROU)

Su-Wei Hsieh & Flavia Pennetta [7]
6/4 6/1

35. Margarita Gasparyan (RUS) & Alexandra Panova (RUS)
36. Ysaline Bonaventure (BEL) & Katalin Marosi (HUN)

Margarita Gasparyan & Alexandra Panova
6/1 4/6 6/2

Su-Wei Hsieh & Flavia Pennetta [7]
6/3 6/4

37. Anna-Lena Groenefeld (GER) & Coco Vandeweghe (USA)
38. Madison Brengle (USA) & Tatjana Maria (GER)

Anna-Lena Groenefeld & Coco Vandeweghe
7/5 6/4

39. Tereza Smitkova (CZE) & Yi-Fan Xu (CHN)
40. **Caroline Garcia** (FRA) & **Katarina Srebotnik** (SLO)...**[10]**

Caroline Garcia & Katarina Srebotnik [10]
6/1 4/6 6/2

Anna-Lena Groenefeld & Coco Vandeweghe
7/6(3) 6/3

Su-Wei Hsieh & Flavia Pennetta [7]
3/6 6/0 9/7

41. **Michaella Krajicek** (NED) & **Barbora Strycova** (CZE)...**[14]**
42. Shuko Aoyama (JPN) & Renata Voracova (CZE)

Michaella Krajicek & Barbora Strycova [14]
7/5 7/5

43. Vera Dushevina (RUS) & Maria Jose Martinez Sanchez (ESP)
44. Klara Koukalova (CZE) & Tsvetana Pironkova (BUL)

Vera Dushevina & Maria Jose Martinez Sanchez
6/2 6/4

Michaella Krajicek & Barbora Strycova [14]
6/3 7/6(7)

45. Karolina Pliskova (CZE) & Kristyna Pliskova (CZE)
46. Monica Niculescu (ROU) & Olga Savchuk (UKR)

Monica Niculescu & Olga Savchuk
2/6 6/4 6/4

Timea Babos & Kristina Mladenovic [4]
6/4 6/2

(Q) 47. Magda Linette (POL) & Mandy Minella (LUX)
48. **Timea Babos** (HUN) & **Kristina Mladenovic** (FRA)...**[4]**

Timea Babos & Kristina Mladenovic [4]
6/4 6/1

Timea Babos & Kristina Mladenovic [4]
6/4 6/4

Timea Babos & Kristina Mladenovic [4]
6/3 4/6 6/4

49. **Garbine Muguruza** (ESP) & **Carla Suarez Navarro** (ESP)...**[6]**
50. Alexandra Dulgheru (ROU) & Silvia Soler-Espinosa (ESP)

Garbine Muguruza & Carla Suarez Navarro [6]
6/4 6/2

51. Cara Black (ZIM) & Lisa Raymond (USA)
(Q) 52. Johanna Larsson (SWE) & Petra Martic (CRO)

Cara Black & Lisa Raymond
5/7 6/3 7/5

Cara Black & Lisa Raymond
6/3 6/1

53. Chen Liang (CHN) & Raluca Olaru (ROU)
54. Belinda Bencic (SUI) & Katerina Siniakova (CZE)

Belinda Bencic & Katerina Siniakova
7/5 7/5

55. Andrea Petkovic (GER) & Magdalena Rybarikova (SVK)
56. **Alla Kudryavtseva** (RUS) & **Anastasia Pavlyuchenkova** (RUS)...**[11]**

Alla Kudryavtseva & Anastasia Pavlyuchenkova [11]
7/5 6/4

Alla Kudryavtseva & Anastasia Pavlyuchenkova [11]
6/1 6/2

Cara Black & Lisa Raymond
2/6 6/3 6/4

Ekaterina Makarova & Elena Vesnina [2]
6/3 4/6 8/6

57. **Anastasia Rodionova** (AUS) & **Arina Rodionova** (AUS)...**[15]**
58. Irina Falconi (USA) & Daria Gavrilova (AUS)

Anastasia Rodionova & Arina Rodionova [15]
6/7(6) 6/2 6/0

59. Timea Bacsinszky (SUI) & Chia-Jung Chuang (TPE)
60. Mona Barthel (GER) & Lyudmyla Kichenok (UKR)

Mona Barthel & Lyudmyla Kichenok
7/5 6/3

Mona Barthel & Lyudmyla Kichenok
6/3 3/6 6/4

61. Lauren Davis (USA) & Kurumi Nara (JPN)
(Q) 62. Yafan Wang (CHN) & Kai-Lin Zhang (CHN)

Lauren Davis & Kurumi Nara
6/4 6/4

Ekaterina Makarova & Elena Vesnina [2]
6/3 6/1

63. Madison Keys (USA) & Laura Robson (GBR)
64. **Ekaterina Makarova** (RUS) & **Elena Vesnina** (RUS)...**[2]**

Ekaterina Makarova & Elena Vesnina [2]
6/4 6/1

Ekaterina Makarova & Elena Vesnina [2]
6/4 6/1

Ekaterina Makarova & Elena Vesnina [2]
6/3 6/1

Quarter-finals / winners column:

Martina Hingis & Sania Mirza [1]

Martina Hingis & Sania Mirza [1]
5/7 7/6(4) 7/5

Timea Babos & Kristina Mladenovic [4]
6/3 4/6 6/4

Ekaterina Makarova & Elena Vesnina [2]
6/3 4/6 6/4

Heavy type denotes seeded players. The figure in brackets against names denotes the order in which they have been seeded.
(WC)=Wild card. (Q)=Qualifier. (LL)=Lucky loser.

EVENT V – THE MIXED DOUBLES CHAMPIONSHIP 2015
Holders: NENAD ZIMONJIC (SER) & SAMANTHA STOSUR (AUS)

The Champions will become the holders, for the year only, of the CHALLENGE CUPS presented by members of the family of the late Mr. S. H. SMITH in 1949 and The All England Lawn Tennis and Croquet Club in 2001.
The Champions will receive a silver three-quarter size replica of the Challenge Cup. A Silver Salver will be presented to each of the Runners-up and a Bronze Medal to each defeated semi-finalist. The matches will be the best of three sets.

First Round	Second Round	Third Round	Quarter-Finals	Semi-Finals	Final

1. Mike Bryan (USA) & Bethanie Mattek-Sands (USA)..[1]
2. Bye
3. Mahesh Bhupathi (IND) & Alla Kudryavtseva (RUS)
4. Nicholas Monroe (USA) & Madison Brengle (USA)..

Mike Bryan & Bethanie Mattek-Sands [1]
Nicholas Monroe & Madison Brengle 5/7 6/3 6/2

Mike Bryan & Bethanie Mattek-Sands [1] 6/4 6/1

(A) 5. Michael Venus (NZL) & Raluca Olaru (ROU)
6. Andre Sa (BRA) & Lara Arruabarrena (ESP)
7. Bye
8. Henri Kontinen (FIN) & Jie Zheng (CHN) ....[15]

Michael Venus & Raluca Olaru 6/3 6/2
Henri Kontinen & Jie Zheng [15]

Michael Venus & Raluca Olaru 6/4 6/2

Mike Bryan & Bethanie Mattek-Sands [1] ....7/6(3) 7/5

9. Juan-Sebastian Cabal (COL) & Cara Black (ZIM)....[9]
10. Bye
(WC) 11. Lleyton Hewitt (AUS) & Casey Dellacqua (AUS)
12. Santiago Gonzalez (MEX) & Abigail Spears (USA)..

Juan-Sebastian Cabal & Cara Black [9]
Lleyton Hewitt & Casey Dellacqua 6/4 6/2

Juan-Sebastian Cabal & Cara Black [9] 0/6 6/3 6/3

13. Aisam Qureshi (PAK) & Vera Dushevina (RUS)
(WC) 14. Ken Skupski (GBR) & Johanna Konta (GBR)
15. Bye
16. Daniel Nestor (CAN) & Kristina Mladenovic (FRA)...[8]

Ken Skupski & Johanna Konta ....7/6(5) 7/5
Daniel Nestor & Kristina Mladenovic [8]

Daniel Nestor & Kristina Mladenovic [8] 5/7 6/1 6/4

Daniel Nestor & Kristina Mladenovic [8] ....6/3 6/7(4) 6/3

Mike Bryan & Bethanie Mattek-Sands [1] ....7/6(2) 6/2

17. Marcin Matkowski (POL) & Elena Vesnina (RUS)...[3]
18. Bye
(WC) 19. Neal Skupski (GBR) & Lisa Raymond (USA)
20. Ivan Dodig (CRO) & Ajla Tomljanovic (AUS)

Marcin Matkowski & Elena Vesnina [3]
Ivan Dodig & Ajla Tomljanovic ....7/6(5) 7/6(4)

Marcin Matkowski & Elena Vesnina [3] 6/4 6/2

21. Jurgen Melzer (AUT) & Barbora Strycova (CZE)
22. Nick Kyrgios (AUS) & Madison Keys (USA)
23. Bye
24. Lukasz Kubot (POL) & Andrea Hlavackova (CZE)..[16]

Nick Kyrgios & Madison Keys ....6/3 7/6(3)
Lukasz Kubot & Andrea Hlavackova [16]

Lukasz Kubot & Andrea Hlavackova [16] ....3/6 7/6(2) 10/8

Marcin Matkowski & Elena Vesnina [3] ....6/7(4) 6/4 11/9

25. Jean-Julien Rojer (NED) & Anna-Lena Groenefeld (GER)...[11]
26. Bye
27. Artem Sitak (NZL) & Anastasia Rodionova (AUS)
(WC) 28. Jonathan Marray (GBR) & Anna Smith (GBR)

Jean-Julien Rojer & Anna-Lena Groenefeld [11]
Artem Sitak & Anastasia Rodionova 6/4 6/4

Artem Sitak & Anastasia Rodionova ....6/4 6/7(1) 6/3

Leander Paes & Martina Hingis [7] 6/2 6/2

29. Adil Shamasdin (CAN) & Gabriela Dabrowski (CAN)
30. Edouard Roger-Vasselin (FRA) & Alize Cornet (FRA)
31. Bye
32. Leander Paes (IND) & Martina Hingis (SUI).....[7]

Edouard Roger-Vasselin & Alize Cornet 6/4 6/3
Leander Paes & Martina Hingis [7]

Leander Paes & Martina Hingis [7] 6/4 6/2

Leander Paes & Martina Hingis [7] 6/2 6/1

Leander Paes & Martina Hingis [7] 6/3 6/4

33. Horia Tecau (ROU) & Katarina Srebotnik (SLO)..[6]
34. Bye
35. Eric Butorac (USA) & Katalin Marosi (HUN)
36. Rohan Bopanna (IND) & Maria Jose Martinez Sanchez (ESP)..

Horia Tecau & Katarina Srebotnik [6]
Rohan Bopanna & Maria Jose Martinez Sanchez ....7/6(9) 5/7 7/5

Horia Tecau & Katarina Srebotnik [6] 6/2 6/4

37. Mariusz Fyrstenberg (POL) & Klaudia Jans-Ignacik (POL)
38. Scott Lipsky (USA) & Hao-Ching Chan (TPE)
39. Bye
40. Raven Klaasen (RSA) & Raquel Kops-Jones (USA)...[10]

Mariusz Fyrstenberg & Klaudia Jans-Ignacik ....6/3 6/7(4) 7/5
Raven Klaasen & Raquel Kops-Jones [10]

Raven Klaasen & Raquel Kops-Jones [10] ....w/o

Horia Tecau & Katarina Srebotnik [6] 6/3 7/5

41. Florin Mergea (ROU) & Michaella Krajicek (NED)..[13]
42. Bye
43. Sergiy Stakhovsky (UKR) & Alicja Rosolska (POL)
44. Robert Lindstedt (SWE) & Anabel Medina Garrigues (ESP)..

Florin Mergea & Michaella Krajicek [13]
Robert Lindstedt & Anabel Medina Garrigues ....7/6(6) 6/2

Robert Lindstedt & Anabel Medina Garrigues 3/6 6/3 6/2

Robert Lindstedt & Anabel Medina Garrigues ....6/4 7/6(3)

45. Nenad Zimonjic (SRB) & Jarmila Gajdosova (AUS)
46. Chris Guccione (AUS) & Andreja Klepac (SLO)
47. Bye
48. Bob Bryan (USA) & Caroline Garcia (FRA).....[4]

Nenad Zimonjic & Jarmila Gajdosova 6/3 7/5
Bob Bryan & Caroline Garcia [4]

Nenad Zimonjic & Jarmila Gajdosova 3/6 6/3 9/7

Robert Lindstedt & Anabel Medina Garrigues 6/4 1/6 6/3

Alexander Peya & Timea Babos [5] 4/6 6/3 11/9

49. Alexander Peya (AUT) & Timea Babos (HUN).....[5]
50. Bye
51. Philipp Oswald (AUT) & Belinda Bencic (SUI)
52. Dominic Inglot (GBR) & Elina Svitolina (UKR)

Alexander Peya & Timea Babos [5]
Philipp Oswald & Belinda Bencic 6/2 6/3

Alexander Peya & Timea Babos [5] ....6/2 6/7(5) 7/5

(A) 53. Oliver Marach (AUT) & Olga Savchuk (UKR)
54. Max Mirnyi (BLR) & Heather Watson (GBR)
55. Bye
56. David Marrero (ESP) & Arantxa Parra Santonja (ESP)..[17]

Oliver Marach & Olga Savchuk ....6/7(5) 7/6(4) 6/4
David Marrero & Arantxa Parra Santonja [17]

Oliver Marach & Olga Savchuk 3/6 6/3 6/2

Alexander Peya & Timea Babos [5] ....6/3 7/6(6)

57. John Peers (AUS) & Yung-Jan Chan (TPE).........[14]
58. Bye
59. Marin Draganja (CRO) & Ana Konjuh (CRO)
(WC) 60. Colin Fleming (GBR) & Jocelyn Rae (GBR)

John Peers & Yung-Jan Chan [14]
Marin Draganja & Ana Konjuh ....6/3 6/7(5) 6/1

Marin Draganja & Ana Konjuh ....7/6(6) 7/6(9)

Alexander Peya & Timea Babos [5] ....3/6 7/6(6) 9/7

61. Rajeev Ram (USA) & Arina Rodionova (AUS)
62. Andre Begemann (GER) & Janette Husarova (SVK)..
63. Bye
64. Bruno Soares (BRA) & Sania Mirza (IND)............[2]

Andre Begemann & Janette Husarova 7/5 6/3
Bruno Soares & Sania Mirza [2]

Bruno Soares & Sania Mirza [2] 6/2 6/4

Bruno Soares & Sania Mirza [2] ....6/3 6/7(5) 6/3

Alexander Peya & Timea Babos [5] 6/1 6/1

Heavy type denotes seeded players. The figure in brackets against names denotes the order in which they have been seeded.
(A)=Alternate. (WC)=Wild card.

EVENT VI – THE BOYS' SINGLES CHAMPIONSHIP 2015
Holder: NOAH RUBIN (USA)

The Champion will become the holder, for the year only, of a Cup presented by The All England Lawn Tennis and Croquet Club. The Champion will receive a three-quarter size Cup and the Runner-up will receive a Silver Salver.
The matches will be best of three sets.

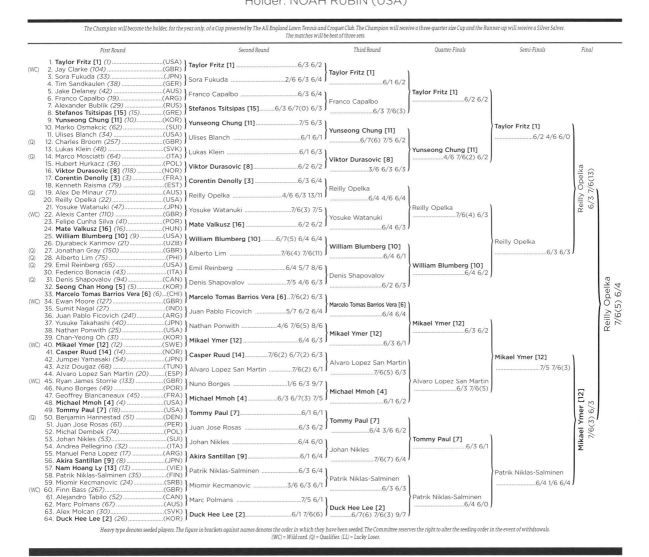

Heavy type denotes seeded players. The figure in brackets against names denotes the order in which they have been seeded. The Committee reserves the right to alter the seeding order in the event of withdrawals. (WC) = Wild card. (Q) = Qualifier. (LL) = Lucky Loser.

EVENT VII – THE BOYS' DOUBLES CHAMPIONSHIP 2015
Holders: ORLANDO LUZ (BRA) & MARCELO ZORMANN (BRA)

The Champions will become the holders, for the year only, of a Cup presented by The All England Lawn Tennis and Croquet Club. The Champions will receive a three-quarter size Cup and the Runners-up will receive a Silver Salvers.
The matches will be best of three sets.

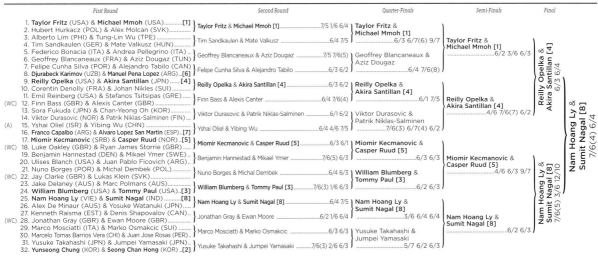

Heavy type denotes seeded players. The figure in brackets against names denotes the order in which they have been seeded. The Committee reserves the right to alter the seeding order in the event of withdrawals. (WC) = Wild card. (Q) = Qualifier. (LL) = Lucky Loser.

WIMBLEDON 2015

EVENT VIII – THE GIRLS' SINGLES CHAMPIONSHIP 2015
Holder: JELENA OSTAPENKO (LAT)

The Champion will become the holder, for the year only, of a Cup presented by The All England Lawn Tennis and Croquet Club. The Champion will receive a three-quarter size Cup and the Runner-up will receive a Silver Salver. The matches will be best of three sets.

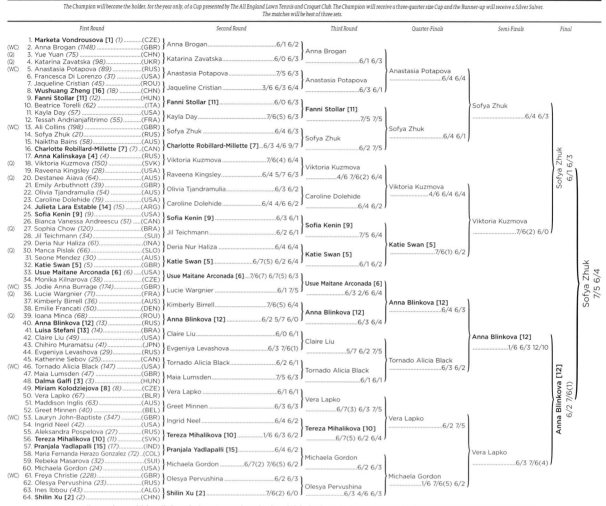

	First Round	Second Round	Third Round	Quarter-Finals	Semi-Finals	Final
	1. **Marketa Vondrousova [1]** *(1)* ....(CZE)	Anna Brogan...........6/1 6/2				
(WC)	2. Anna Brogan *(1148)* ....(GBR)		Anna Brogan			
(Q)	3. Yue Yuan *(75)* ....(CHN)	Katarina Zavatska.........6/0 6/3	...........6/1 6/3			
(Q)	4. Katarina Zavatska *(98)* ....(UKR)			Anastasia Potapova		
(WC)	5. Anastasia Potapova *(89)* ....(RUS)	Anastasia Potapova.........7/5 6/3		...........6/4 6/4		
	6. Francesca Di Lorenzo *(31)* ....(USA)		Anastasia Potapova			
	7. Jaqueline Cristian *(45)* ....(ROU)	Jaqueline Cristian.........3/6 6/3 6/4	...........6/3 6/1			
	8. **Wushuang Zheng [16]** *(18)* ....(CHN)				Sofya Zhuk	
	9. **Fanni Stollar [11]** *(12)* ....(HUN)	Fanni Stollar [11].........6/0 6/3			...........6/4 6/3	
	10. Beatrice Torelli *(62)* ....(ITA)		Fanni Stollar [11]			
	11. Kayla Day *(57)* ....(USA)	Kayla Day.........7/6(5) 6/2	...........7/5 7/5			
	12. Tessah Andrianjafitrimo *(55)* ....(FRA)			Sofya Zhuk		
(WC)	13. Ali Collins *(198)* ....(GBR)	Sofya Zhuk.........6/4 6/3		...........6/4 6/1		
	14. Sofya Zhuk *(21)* ....(RUS)		Sofya Zhuk			
	15. Naiktha Bains *(58)* ....(AUS)	Charlotte Robillard-Millette [7]...6/3 4/6 9/7	...........6/2 7/5			
	16. **Charlotte Robillard-Millette [7]** *(7)* ..(CAN)					Sofya Zhuk
	17. **Anna Kalinskaya [4]** *(4)* ....(RUS)	Viktoria Kuzmova.........7/6(4) 6/4				6/1 6/3
(Q)	18. Viktoria Kuzmova *(150)* ....(SVK)		Viktoria Kuzmova			
	19. Raveena Kingsley *(28)* ....(USA)	Raveena Kingsley.........6/4 5/7 6/2	...........4/6 7/6(2) 6/4			
(Q)	20. Destanee Aiava *(64)* ....(AUS)			Viktoria Kuzmova		
	21. Emily Arbuthnott *(39)* ....(GBR)	Olivia Tjandramulia.........6/3 6/2		...........4/6 6/4 6/4		
	22. Olivia Tjandramulia *(54)* ....(AUS)		Caroline Dolehide			
	23. Caroline Dolehide *(19)* ....(USA)	Caroline Dolehide.........6/4 4/6 6/2	...........6/4 6/2			
	24. **Julieta Lara Estable [14]** *(15)* ...(ARG)				Viktoria Kuzmova	
	25. **Sofia Kenin [9]** *(9)* ....(USA)	Sofia Kenin [9].........6/3 6/1			...........7/6(2) 6/0	
	26. Bianca Vanessa Andreescu *(51)* ....(CAN)		Sofia Kenin [9]			
(Q)	27. Sophia Chow *(120)* ....(BRA)	Jil Teichmann.........6/2 6/1	...........7/5 6/4			
(Q)	28. Jil Teichmann *(34)* ....(SUI)			Katie Swan [5]		
	29. Deria Nur Haliza *(61)* ....(INA)	Deria Nur Haliza.........6/4 6/4		...........7/6(1) 6/2		
(Q)	30. Manca Pislak *(66)* ....(SLO)		Katie Swan [5]			
	31. Seone Mendez *(30)* ....(AUS)	Katie Swan [5].........6/7(5) 6/2 6/4	...........6/1 6/2			
	32. **Katie Swan [5]** *(5)* ....(GBR)					
	33. **Usue Maitane Arconada [6]** *(6)* ....(USA)	Usue Maitane Arconada [6]...7/6(7) 6/7(5) 6/3				
	34. Monika Kilnarova *(38)* ....(CZE)		Usue Maitane Arconada [6]			
(WC)	35. Jodie Anna Burrage *(174)* ....(GBR)	Lucie Wargnier.........6/1 7/5	...........6/3 2/6 6/4			
(Q)	36. Lucie Wargnier *(71)* ....(FRA)			Anna Blinkova [12]		
	37. Kimberly Birrell *(36)* ....(AUS)	Kimberly Birrell.........7/6(5) 6/4		...........6/4 6/3		
	38. Emilie Francati *(50)* ....(DEN)		Anna Blinkova [12]			
(Q)	39. Ioana Minca *(68)* ....(ROU)	Anna Blinkova [12].........6/2 5/7 6/0	...........6/3 6/4			
	40. **Anna Blinkova [12]** *(13)* ....(RUS)				Anna Blinkova [12]	
	41. **Luisa Stefani [13]** *(14)* ....(BRA)	Claire Liu.........6/0 6/1			...........1/6 6/3 12/10	
	42. Claire Liu *(49)* ....(USA)		Claire Liu			
	43. Chihiro Muramatsu *(41)* ....(JPN)	Evgeniya Levashova.........6/3 7/6(1)	...........5/7 6/2 7/5			
	44. Evgeniya Levashova *(29)* ....(RUS)			Tornado Alicia Black		
	45. Katherine Sebov *(25)* ....(CAN)	Tornado Alicia Black.........6/2 6/1		...........6/3 6/2		
(WC)	46. Tornado Alicia Black *(147)* ....(USA)		Tornado Alicia Black			
	47. Maia Lumsden *(47)* ....(GBR)	Maia Lumsden.........7/5 6/3	...........6/1 6/1			Anna Blinkova [12]
	48. **Dalma Galfi [3]** *(3)* ....(HUN)					6/2 7/6(1)
	49. **Miriam Kolodziejova [8]** *(8)* ......(CZE)	Vera Lapko.........6/1 6/1				
	50. Vera Lapko *(67)* ....(BLR)		Vera Lapko			
	51. Maddison Inglis *(63)* ....(AUS)	Greet Minnen.........6/3 6/3	...........6/7(3) 6/3 7/5			
	52. Greet Minnen *(40)* ....(BEL)			Vera Lapko		
(WC)	53. Lauryn John-Baptiste *(347)* ....(GBR)	Ingrid Neel.........6/4 6/2		...........6/2 7/5		
	54. Ingrid Neel *(42)* ....(USA)		Tereza Mihalikova [10]			
	55. Aleksandra Pospelova *(27)* ....(RUS)	Tereza Mihalikova [10]...1/6 6/3 6/2	...........6/7(5) 6/2 6/4			
	56. **Tereza Mihalikova [10]** *(11)* ......(SVK)				Vera Lapko	
	57. **Pranjala Yadlapalli [15]** *(17)* ....(IND)	Pranjala Yadlapalli [15].........6/4 6/2			...........6/3 7/6(4)	
	58. Maria Fernanda Herazo Gonzalez *(72)* .(COL)		Michaela Gordon			
	59. Rebeka Masarova *(32)* ....(SUI)	Michaela Gordon.........6/7(2) 7/6(5) 6/2	...........6/2 6/3			
	60. Michaela Gordon *(24)* ....(USA)			Michaela Gordon		
(WC)	61. Freya Christie *(228)* ....(GBR)	Olesya Pervushina.........6/2 6/3		...........1/6 7/6(5) 6/2		
	62. Olesya Pervushina *(23)* ....(RUS)		Olesya Pervushina			
	63. Ines Ibbou *(43)* ....(ALG)	Shilin Xu [2].........7/6(2) 6/0	...........6/3 4/6 6/3			
	64. **Shilin Xu [2]** *(2)* ....(CHN)					

Heavy type denotes seeded players. The figure in brackets against names denotes the order in which they have been seeded. The Committee reserves the right to alter the seeding order in the event of withdrawals.
(WC) = Wild card. (Q) = Qualifier. (LL) = Lucky Loser.

EVENT IX – THE GIRLS' DOUBLES CHAMPIONSHIP 2015
Holders: TAMI GRENDE (IND) & QIU YU YE (CHI)

The Champions will become the holders, for the year only, of a Cup presented by The All England Lawn Tennis and Croquet Club. The Champions will receive a three-quarter size Cup and the Runners-up will receive a Silver Salvers. The matches will be best of three sets.

	First Round	Second Round	Quarter-Finals	Semi-Finals	Final
	1. Miriam Kolodziejova (CZE) & **Marketa Vondrousova** (CZE)...[1]	Miriam Kolodziejova & Marketa Vondrousova [1]..6/1 6/0	Miriam Kolodziejova & Marketa Vondrousova [1]		
	2. Jaqueline Cristian (ROU) & Sofia Kenin (USA)		...........6/4 6/2	Miriam Kolodziejova & Marketa Vondrousova [1]	
	3. Bianca Vanessa Andreescu (CAN) & Katherine Sebov (CAN)...	Bianca Vanessa Andreescu & Katherine Sebov ..6/0 6/2		...........6/3 6/1	
(WC)	4. Georgina Axon (GBR) & Holly Hutchinson (GBR)...				
	5. Chihiro Muramatsu (JPN) & Pranjala Yadlapalli (IND)...	Maria Fernanda Herazo Gonzalez & Deria Nur Haliza ..6/3 6/2	Anna Blinkova & Olesya Pervushina [7]		
	6. Maria Fernanda Herazo Gonzalez (COL) & Deria Nur Haliza (INA)...		...........6/3 6/4		
	7. Sophia Chow (BRA) & Yue Yuan (CHN)......................	Anna Blinkova & Olesya Pervushina [7]..6/0 6/2			Dalma Galfi & Fanni Stollar [3]
	8. **Anna Blinkova** (RUS) & **Olesya Pervushina** (RUS) ..[7]				7/6(2) 6/4
	9. **Dalma Galfi** (HUN) & **Fanni Stollar** (HUN)............[3]	Dalma Galfi & Fanni Stollar [3]...........6/2 6/1	Dalma Galfi & Fanni Stollar [3]		
(WC)	10. Jasmine Amber Asghar (GBR) & Eden Richardson (GBR)...		...........7/5 6/3	Dalma Galfi & Fanni Stollar [3]	
	11. Eleni Christofi (GRE) & Lesedi Sheya Jacobs (NAM)...	Karola Patricia Bejenaru & Panna Udvardy ..6/2 6/1		...........6/0 6/2	
	12. Karola Patricia Bejenaru (ROU) & Panna Udvardy (HUN)...				
	13. Kimberly Birrell (AUS) & Maddison Inglis (AUS)...	Michaela Gordon & Claire Liu...........6/4 6/2	Maia Lumsden & Ingrid Neel		
	14. Michaela Gordon (USA) & Claire Liu (USA)...............		...........6/3 6/2		
	15. Maia Lumsden (GBR) & Ingrid Neel (USA).................	Maia Lumsden & Ingrid Neel...........6/3 7/5			
	16. **Julieta Lara Estable** (ARG) & **Wushuang Zheng** (CHN)..[5]				Dalma Galfi & Fanni Stollar [3]
	17. **Francesca Di Lorenzo** (USA) & **Luisa Stefani** (BRA)..[8]	Francesca Di Lorenzo & Luisa Stefani [8] ..3/6 7/5 6/1	Destanee Aiava & Olivia Tjandramulia		6/3 6/2
(WC)	18. Jodie Anna Burrage (GBR) & Ali Collins (GBR)...		...........4/6 7/6(3) 6/3		
	19. Destanee Aiava (AUS) & Olivia Tjandramulia (AUS)...	Destanee Aiava & Olivia Tjandramulia ..6/2 6/1		Vera Lapko & Tereza Mihalikova	
	20. Ines Ibbou (ALG) & Katarina Zavatska (UKR)			...........3/6 6/3 6/1	
	21. Vera Lapko (BLR) & Tereza Mihalikova (SVK)...	Vera Lapko & Tereza Mihalikova ....6/2 7/6(4)	Vera Lapko & Tereza Mihalikova		
	22. Tessah Andrianjafitrimo (FRA) & Seone Mendez (AUS)...		...........7/5 6/1		
	23. Kayla Day (USA) & Monika Kilnarova (CZE)...	Kayla Day & Monika Kilnarova ....6/3 7/6(7)			Vera Lapko & Tereza Mihalikova
	24. **Anna Kalinskaya** (RUS) & **Evgeniya Levashova** (RUS) ..[4]				6/4 7/5
	25. **Jil Teichmann** (SUI) & **Shilin Xu** (CHN)..............[6]	Jil Teichmann & Shilin Xu [6]...........2/6 6/4 6/4	Jil Teichmann & Shilin Xu [6]		
	26. Aleksandra Pospelova (RUS) & Sofya Zhuk (RUS)..[2]		...........6/4 7/5	Anna Brogan & Freya Christie	
	27. Naiktha Bains (AUS) & Tornado Alicia Black (USA)...	Naiktha Bains & Tornado Alicia Black 6/1 6/4		...........6/4 7/5	
	28. Emily Arbuthnott (GBR) & Emilie Francati (DEN)...				
(WC)	29. Anna Brogan (GBR) & Freya Christie (GBR)...	Anna Brogan & Freya Christie 6/3 3/6 6/2	Anna Brogan & Freya Christie		
	30. Viktoria Kuzmova (SVK) & Beatrice Torelli (ITA)...				
	31. Ioana Minca (ROU) & Manca Pislak (SLO)...	Usue Maitane Arconada & Charlotte Robillard-Millette [2]..7/6(5) 6/1	...........7/5 6/2		
	32. **Usue Maitane Arconada** (USA) & **Charlotte Robillard-Millette** (CAN)..[2]				

Heavy type denotes seeded players. The figure in brackets against names denotes the order in which they have been seeded. The Committee reserves the right to alter the seeding order in the event of withdrawals.
(WC) = Wild card. (Q) = Qualifier. (LL) = Lucky Loser.

EVENT X – THE GENTLEMEN'S INVITATION DOUBLES 2015
Holders: THOMAS ENQVIST (SWE) & MARK PHILIPPOUSSIS (AUS)

The Champions will become the holders, for the year only, of a Cup presented by The All England Lawn Tennis and Croquet Club. The Champions will receive a silver three-quarter size Cup. A Silver Medal will be presented to each of the Runners-up. The matches will be the best of three sets. If a match should reach one set all a 10 point tie-break will replace the third set.

GROUP A	Albert Costa (ESP) & Fernando Gonzalez (CHI)	Wayne Ferreira (RSA) & Sebastien Grosjean (FRA)	Richard Krajicek (NED) & Mark Petchey (GBR)	Jamie Baker (GBR) & Fabrice Santoro (FRA)	Wins	Losses	Final
Albert Costa (ESP) & Fernando Gonzalez (CHI)		6/7(1) 7/6(5) [5-10] L	4/6 6/1 [10-5] W	1/6 6/2 [9-11] L	1	2	
Wayne Ferreira (RSA) & Sebastien Grosjean (FRA)	7/6(1) 6/7(5) [10-5] W		6/3 6/4 W	3/6 4/6 L	2	1	Wayne Ferreira & Sebastien Grosjean
Richard Krajicek (NED) & Mark Petchey (GBR)	6/4 1/6 [5-10] L	3/6 4/6 L		5/7 5/7 L	0	3	
Jamie Baker (GBR) & Fabrice Santoro (FRA)	6/1 2/6 [11-9] W	6/3 6/4 W	* 7/5 7/5		2	0	

*Greg Rusedski withdrew (ankle injury) after first match and was replaced by Jamie Baker. This result does not count towards total matches won.

GROUP B	Jonas Bjorkman (SWE) & Thomas Johansson (SWE)	Jamie Delgado (GBR) & Thomas Enqvist (SWE)	Justin Gimelstob (USA) & Ross Hutchins (GBR)	Goran Ivanisevic (CRO) & Ivan Ljubicic (CRO)	Wins	Losses	Final
Jonas Bjorkman (SWE) & Thomas Johansson (SWE)		6/3 7/6(4) W	6/3 2/6 [3-10] L	1/6 6/1 [7-10] L	1	2	
Jamie Delgado (GBR) & Thomas Enqvist (SWE)	3/6 6/7(4) L		3/6 6/2 [7-10] L	6/3 1/6 [8-10] L	0	3	Goran Ivanisevic & Ivan Ljubicic
Justin Gimelstob (USA) & Ross Hutchins (GBR)	3/6 6/2 [10-3] W	6/3 2/6 [10-7] W		4/6 6/2 [6-10] L	2	1	
Goran Ivanisevic (CRO) & Ivan Ljubicic (CRO)	6/1 1/6 [10-7] W	3/6 6/1 [10-8] W	6/4 2/6 [10-6] W		3	0	

Overall Final: Goran Ivanisevic & Ivan Ljubicic 6/3 1/6 [10-5]

This event consists of eight invited pairs divided into two groups, playing each other within their group on a 'round robin' basis. The group winner is the pair with the highest number of wins. In the case of a tie the winning pair may be determined by head to head results or a formula based on percentage of sets/games won to those played.

EVENT XI – THE GENTLEMEN'S SENIOR INVITATION DOUBLES 2015
Holders: GUY FORGET (FRA) & CEDRIC PIOLINE (FRA)

The Champions will become the holders, for the year only, of a Cup presented by The All England Lawn Tennis and Croquet Club. The Champions will receive a silver half-size Cup. A Silver Medal will be presented to each of the Runners-up. The matches will be the best of three sets. If a match should reach one set all a 10 point tie-break will replace the third set.

GROUP A	Mansour Bahrami (IRI) & Henri Leconte (FRA)	Andrew Castle (GBR) & Jeff Tarango (USA)	Jacco Eltingh (NED) & Paul Haarhuis (NED)	Todd Woodbridge (AUS) & Mark Woodforde (AUS)	Wins	Losses	Final
Mansour Bahrami (IRI) & Henri Leconte (FRA)		3/6 7/5 [7-10] L	4/6 5/7 L	3/6 6/7(3) L	0	3	
Andrew Castle (GBR) & Jeff Tarango (USA)	6/3 5/7 [10-7] W		2/6 6/7(1) L	4/6 7/6(5) [13-11] W	2	1	Jacco Eltingh & Paul Haarhuis
Jacco Eltingh (NED) & Paul Haarhuis (NED)	6/4 7/5 W	6/2 7/6(1) W		7/5 6/4 W	3	0	
Todd Woodbridge (AUS) & Mark Woodforde (AUS)	6/3 7/6(3) W	6/4 6/7(5) [11-13] L	5/7 4/6 L		1	2	

GROUP B	Jeremy Bates (GBR) & Chris Wilkinson (GBR)	Guy Forget (FRA) & Cedric Pioline (FRA)	Rick Leach (USA) & Patrick McEnroe (USA)	Joakim Nystrom (SWE) & Mikael Pernfors (SWE)	Wins	Losses	Final
Jeremy Bates (GBR) & Chris Wilkinson (GBR)		1/6 6/3 [10-4] W	3/6 2/6 L	7/5 6/1 W	2	1	
Guy Forget (FRA) & Cedric Pioline (FRA)	6/1 3/6 [4-10] L		6/3 6/2 W	6/3 6/3 W	2	1	Guy Forget & Cedric Pioline
Rick Leach (USA) & Patrick McEnroe (USA)	6/3 6/2 W	3/6 2/6 L		6/2 7/5 W	2	1	
Joakim Nystrom (SWE) & Mikael Pernfors (SWE)	5/7 1/6 L	3/6 3/6 L	2/6 5/7 L		0	3	

Overall Final: Jacco Eltingh & Paul Haarhuis 6/4 6/4

This event consists of eight invited pairs divided into two groups, playing each other within their group on a 'round robin' basis. The group winner is the pair with the highest number of wins. In the case of a tie the winning pair may be determined by head to head results or a formula based on percentage of sets/games won to those played.

ALPHABETICAL LIST – INVITATION DOUBLES EVENTS
GENTLEMEN

Baker, Jamie (Great Britain)
Bjorkman, Jonas (Sweden)
Costa, Albert (Spain)
Delgado, Jamie (Great Britain)
Enqvist, Thomas (Sweden)
Ferreira, Wayne (South Africa)
Gimelstob, Justin (USA)
Gonzalez, Fernando (Chile)
Grosjean, Sebastien (France)
Hutchins, Ross (Great Britain)
Ivanisevic, Goran (Croatia)
Johansson, Thomas (Sweden)
Krajicek, Richard (Netherlands)
Ljubicic, Ivan (Croatia)
Petchey, Mark (Great Britain)
Santoro, Fabrice (France)

LADIES

Austin, Tracy (USA)
Bartoli, Marion (France)
Davenport, Lindsay (USA)
Fernandez, Mary Joe (USA)
Jaeger, Andrea (USA)
Majoli, Iva (Croatia)
Maleeva, Magdalena (Bulgaria)
Navratilova, Martina (USA)
Novotna, Jana (Czech Republic)
Rubin, Chanda (USA)
Schett, Barbara (Austria)
Sfar, Selima (Tunisia)
Stubbs, Rennae (Australia)
Sukova, Helena (Czech Republic)
Temesvari, Andrea (Hungary)
Testud, Sandrine (France)

ALPHABETICAL LIST – GENTLEMEN'S SENIOR INVITATION DOUBLES EVENTS

Bahrami, Mansour (Iran)
Bates, Jeremy (Great Britain)
Castle, Andrew (Great Britain)
Eltingh, Jacco (Netherlands)
Forget, Guy (France)
Haarhuis, Paul (Netherlands)
Leach, Rick (USA)
Leconte, Henri (France)
McEnroe, Patrick (USA)
Nystrom, Joakim (Sweden)
Pernfors, Mikael (Sweden)
Pioline, Cedric (France)
Tarango, Jeff (USA)
Wilkinson, Chris (Great Britain)
Woodbridge, Todd (Australia)
Woodforde, Mark (Australia)

EVENT XII – THE LADIES' INVITATION DOUBLES 2015
Holders: JANA NOVOTNA (CZE) & BARBARA SCHETT (AUT)

The Champions will become the holders, for the year only, of a Cup presented by The All England Lawn Tennis and Croquet Club. The Champions will receive a silver three-quarter size Cup. A Silver Medal will be presented to each of the Runners-up. The matches will be the best of three sets. If a match should reach one set all a 10 point tie-break will replace the third set.

GROUP A	Tracy Austin (USA) & Helena Sukova (CZE)	Marion Bartoli (FRA) & Iva Majoli (CRO)	Lindsay Davenport (USA) & Mary Joe Fernandez (USA)	Martina Navratilova (USA) & Selima Sfar (TUN)	Results Wins	Results Losses	Final
Tracy Austin (USA) & Helena Sukova (CZE)		w/o L	2/6 4/6 L	2/6 2/6 L	0	3	
Marion Bartoli (FRA) & Iva Majoli (CRO)	w/o W		2/6 7/5 [2-10] L	6/7(3) 4/6 L	1	2	Martina Navratilova & Selima Sfar
Lindsay Davenport (USA) & Mary Joe Fernandez (USA)	6/2 6/4 W	6/2 5/7 [10-2] W		4/6 1/6 L	2	1	
Martina Navratilova (USA) & Selima Sfar (TUN)	6/2 6/2 W	7/6(3) 6/4 W	6/4 6/1 W		3	0	

GROUP B	Andrea Jaeger (USA) & Andrea Temesvari (HUN)	Magdalena Maleeva (BUL) & Rennae Stubbs (AUS)	Jana Novotna (CZE) & Barbara Schett (AUT)	Chanda Rubin (USA) & Sandrine Testud (FRA)	Results Wins	Results Losses	
Andrea Jaeger (USA) & Andrea Temesvari (HUN)		4/6 3/6 L	1/6 5/7 L	6/7(2) 4/6 L	0	3	Magdalena Maleeva & Rennae Stubbs
Magdalena Maleeva (BUL) & Rennae Stubbs (AUS)	6/4 6/3 W		7/6(6) 6/3 W	4/6 6/3 [13-11] W	3	0	
Jana Novotna (CZE) & Barbara Schett (AUT)	6/1 7/5 W	6/7(6) 3/6 L		4/6 6/3 [8-10] L	1	2	
Chanda Rubin (USA) & Sandrine Testud (FRA)	7/6(2) 6/4 W	6/4 3/6 [11-13] L	6/4 3/6 [10-8] W		2	1	

Final: Martina Navratilova & Selima Sfar — Magdalena Maleeva & Rennae Stubbs 3/6 7/5 [10-8]

This event consists of eight invited pairs divided into two groups, playing each other within their group on a 'round robin' basis. The group winner is the pair with the highest number of wins. In the case of a tie the winning pair may be determined by head to head results or a formula based on percentage of sets/games won to those played.

EVENT XIII – THE WHEELCHAIR GENTLEMEN'S DOUBLES 2015
Holders: STEPHANE HOUDET (FRA) & SHINGO KUNIEDA (JPN)

The Champions will become the holders, for one year only, of a Cup presented by The All England Lawn and Croquet Club. The Champions will receive a Silver Salver. The Runners-up will each receive a Silver Medal. The matches will be the best of three tie-break sets.

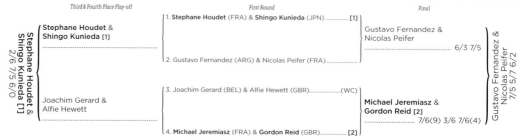

Third & Fourth Place Play-off — Stephane Houdet & Shingo Kunieda [1] — Joachim Gerard & Alfie Hewett — Stephane Houdet & Shingo Kunieda [1] 2/6 7/5 6/0

First Round
1. **Stephane Houdet** (FRA) & **Shingo Kunieda** (JPN) .... **[1]**
2. Gustavo Fernandez (ARG) & Nicolas Peifer (FRA) ....
3. Joachim Gerard (BEL) & Alfie Hewett (GBR)....................(WC)
4. **Michael Jeremiasz** (FRA) & **Gordon Reid** (GBR)................ **[2]**

Gustavo Fernandez & Nicolas Peifer 6/3 7/5
Michael Jeremiasz & Gordon Reid [2] .... 7/6(9) 3/6 7/6(4)

Final: Gustavo Fernandez & Nicolas Peifer 7/5 5/7 6/2

Heavy type denotes seeded players. The figure in brackets against names denotes the order in which they have been seeded.

EVENT XIV – THE WHEELCHAIR LADIES' DOUBLES 2015
Holders: YUI KAMIJI (JPN) & JORDANNE WHILEY (GBR)

The Champions will become the holders, for one year only, of a Cup presented by The All England Lawn and Croquet Club. The Champions will receive a Silver Salver. The Runners-up will each receive a Silver Medal. The matches will be the best of three tie-break sets.

Third & Fourth Place Play-off — Louise Hunt (GBR) & Katharina Kruger — Sabine Ellerbrock & Lucy Shuker — Sabine Ellerbrock & Lucy Shuker 6/1 6/1

First Round
1. **Yui Kamiji** (JPN) & **Jordanne Whiley** (GBR) .... **[1]**
2. Louise Hunt (GBR) & Katharina Kruger (GER)................(WC)
3. Sabine Ellerbrock (GER) & Lucy Shuker (GBR)...........................
4. **Jiske Griffioen** (NED) & **Aniek Van Koot** (NED).................. **[2]**

Yui Kamiji & Jordanne Whiley [1] 6/0 6/3
Jiske Griffioen & Aniek Van Koot [2] 6/2 6/4

Final: Yui Kamiji & Jordanne Whiley [1] 6/2 5/7 6/3

Heavy type denotes seeded players. The figure in brackets against names denotes the order in which they have been seeded.

ROLLS OF HONOUR
GENTLEMEN'S SINGLES CHAMPIONS & RUNNERS-UP

	1877	S.W.Gore *W.C.Marshall*	1903	H.L.Doherty *F.L.Riseley*	1933	J.H.Crawford *H.E.Vines*	1965	R.S.Emerson *F.S.Stolle*	1991 M.D.Stich *B.F.Becker*
	1878	P.F.Hadow *S.W.Gore*	1904	H.L.Doherty *F.L.Riseley*	1934	F.J.Perry *J.H.Crawford*	1966	M.M.Santana *R.D.Ralston*	1992 A.K.Agassi *G.S.Ivanisevic*
*	1879	J.T.Hartley *V.T.St.L.Goold*	1905	H.L.Doherty *N.E.Brookes*	1935	F.J.Perry *G.von Cramm*	1967	J.D.Newcombe *W.P.Bungert*	1993 P.Sampras *J.S.Courier*
	1880	J.T.Hartley *H.F.Lawford*	1906	H.L.Doherty *F.L.Riseley*	1936	F.J.Perry *G.von Cramm*	1968	R.G.Laver *A.D.Roche*	1994 P.Sampras *G.S.Ivanisevic*
	1881	W.C.Renshaw *J.T.Hartley*	* 1907	N.E.Brookes *A.W.Gore*	* 1937	J.D.Budge *G.von Cramm*	1969	R.G.Laver *J.D.Newcombe*	1995 P.Sampras *B.F.Becker*
	1882	W.C.Renshaw *J.E.Renshaw*	* 1908	A.W.Gore *H.R.Barrett*	1938	J.D.Budge *H.W.Austin*	1970	J.D.Newcombe *K.R.Rosewall*	1996 R.P.S.Krajicek *M.O.Washington*
	1883	W.C.Renshaw *J.E.Renshaw*	1909	A.W.Gore *M.J.G.Ritchie*	* 1939	R.L.Riggs *E.T.Cooke*	1971	J.D.Newcombe *S.R.Smith*	1997 P.Sampras *C.A.Pioline*
	1884	W.C.Renshaw *H.F.Lawford*	1910	A.F.Wilding *A.W.Gore*	* 1946	Y.F.M.Petra *G.E.Brown*	* 1972	S.R.Smith *I.Nastase*	1998 P.Sampras *G.S.Ivanisevic*
	1885	W.C.Renshaw *H.F.Lawford*	1911	A.F.Wilding *H.R.Barrett*	1947	J.A.Kramer *T.P.Brown*	* 1973	J.Kodes *A.Metreveli*	1999 P.Sampras *A.K.Agassi*
	1886	W.C.Renshaw *H.F.Lawford*	1912	A.F.Wilding *A.W.Gore*	* 1948	R.Falkenburg *J.E.Bromwich*	1974	J.S.Connors *K.R.Rosewall*	2000 P.Sampras *P.M.Rafter*
*	1887	H.F.Lawford *J.E.Renshaw*	1913	A.F.Wilding *M.E.McLoughlin*	1949	F.R.Schroeder *J.Drobny*	1975	A.R.Ashe *J.S.Connors*	2001 G.Ivanisevic *P.M.Rafter*
	1888	J.E.Renshaw *H.F.Lawford*	1914	N.E.Brookes *A.F.Wilding*	* 1950	J.E.Patty *F.A.Sedgman*	1976	B.R.Borg *I.Nastase*	2002 L.G.Hewitt *D.P.Nalbandian*
	1889	W.C.Renshaw *J.E.Renshaw*	1919	G.L.Patterson *N.E.Brookes*	1951	R.Savitt *K.B.McGregor*	1977	B.R.Borg *J.S.Connors*	2003 R.Federer *M.A.Philippoussis*
	1890	W.J.Hamilton *W.C.Renshaw*	1920	W.T.Tilden *G.L.Patterson*	1952	F.A.Sedgman *J.Drobny*	1978	B.R.Borg *J.S.Connors*	2004 R.Federer *A.S.Roddick*
*	1891	W.Baddeley *J.Pim*	1921	W.T.Tilden *B.I.C.Norton*	* 1953	E.V.Seixas *K.Nielsen*	1979	B.R.Borg *L.R.Tanner*	2005 R.Federer *A.S.Roddick*
	1892	W.Baddeley *J.Pim*	*† 1922	G.L.Patterson *R.Lycett*	1954	J.Drobny *K.R.Rosewall*	1980	B.Borg *J.P.McEnroe*	2006 R.Federer *R.Nadal*
	1893	J.Pim *W.Baddeley*	* 1923	W.M.Johnston *F.T.Hunter*	1955	M.A.Trabert *K.Nielsen*	1981	J.P.McEnroe *B.R.Borg*	2007 R.Federer *R.Nadal*
	1894	J.Pim *W.Baddeley*	* 1924	J.R.Borotra *J.R.Lacoste*	* 1956	L.A.Hoad *K.R.Rosewall*	1982	J.S.Connors *J.P.McEnroe*	2008 R.Nadal *R.Federer*
*	1895	W.Baddeley *W.V.Eaves*	1925	J.R.Lacoste *J.R.Borotra*	1957	L.A.Hoad *A.J.Cooper*	1983	J.P.McEnroe *C.J.Lewis*	2009 R.Federer *A.S.Roddick*
	1896	H.S.Mahony *W.Baddeley*	* 1926	J.R.Borotra *H.O.Kinsey*	* 1958	A.J.Cooper *N.A.Fraser*	1984	J.P.McEnroe *J.S.Connors*	2010 R.Nadal *T.Berdych*
	1897	R.F.Doherty *H.S.Mahony*	1927	H.J.Cochet *J.R.Borotra*	* 1959	A.R.Olmedo *R.G.Laver*	1985	B.F.Becker *K.M.Curren*	2011 N.Djokovic *R.Nadal*
	1898	R.F.Doherty *H.L.Doherty*	1928	J.R.Lacoste *H.J.Cochet*	* 1960	N.A.Fraser *R.G.Laver*	1986	B.F.Becker *I.Lendl*	2012 R.Federer *A.B.Murray*
	1899	R.F.Doherty *A.W.Gore*	* 1929	H.J.Cochet *J.R.Borotra*	1961	R.G.Laver *C.R.McKinley*	1987	P.H.Cash *I.Lendl*	2013 A.B.Murray *N.Djokovic*
	1900	R.F.Doherty *S.H.Smith*	1930	W.T.Tilden *W.L.Allison*	1962	R.G.Laver *M.F.Mulligan*	1988	S.B.Edberg *B.F.Becker*	2014 N.Djokovic *R.Federer*
	1901	A.W.Gore *R.F.Doherty*	* 1931	S.B.B.Wood *F.X.Shields*	* 1963	C.R.McKinley *F.S.Stolle*	1989	B.F.Becker *S.B.Edberg*	2015 N.Djokovic *R.Federer*
	1902	H.L.Doherty *A.W.Gore*	1932	H.E.Vines *H.W.Austin*	1964	R.S.Emerson *F.S.Stolle*	1990	S.B.Edberg *B.F.Becker*	

For the years 1913, 1914 and 1919-1923 inclusive the above records include the 'World's Championships on Grass' granted to The Lawn Tennis Association by The International Lawn Tennis Federation.
This title was then abolished and commencing in 1924 they became The Official Lawn Tennis Championships recognised by The International Lawn Tennis Federation.
Prior to 1922 the holders in the Singles Events and Gentlemen's Doubles did not compete in The Championships but met the winners of these events in the Challenge Rounds.
† Challenge Round abolished: holders subsequently played through.
* The holder did not defend the title.

LADIES' SINGLES CHAMPIONS & RUNNERS-UP

Year	Champion / Runner-up	Year	Champion / Runner-up	Year	Champion / Runner-up	Year	Champion / Runner-up	Year	Champion / Runner-up
1884	Miss M.E.E.Watson / *Miss L.M.Watson*	1910	Mrs.R.L.Chambers / *Miss P.D.H.Boothby*	*1946	Miss P.M.Betz / *Miss A.L.Brough*	1972	Mrs.L.W.King / *Miss E.F.Goolagong*	*1997	Miss M.Hingis / *Miss J.Novotna*
1885	Miss M.E.E.Watson / *Miss B.Bingley*	1911	Mrs.R.L.Chambers / *Miss P.D.H.Boothby*	*1947	Miss M.E.Osborne / *Miss D.J.Hart*	1973	Mrs.L.W.King / *Miss C.M.Evert*	1998	Miss J.Novotna / *Miss N.Tauziat*
1886	Miss B.Bingley / *Miss M.E.E.Watson*	*1912	Mrs.D.T.R.Larcombe / *Mrs.A.Sterry*	1948	Miss A.L.Brough / *Miss D.J.Hart*	1974	Miss C.M.Evert / *Mrs.O.V.Morozova*	1999	Miss L.A.Davenport / *Miss S.M.Graf*
1887	Miss C.Dod / *Miss B.Bingley*	*1913	Mrs.R.L.Chambers / *Mrs.R.J.McNair*	1949	Miss A.L.Brough / *Mrs.W.du Pont*	1975	Mrs.L.W.King / *Mrs.R.A.Cawley*	2000	Miss V.E.S.Williams / *Miss L.A.Davenport*
1888	Miss C.Dod / *Mrs.G.W.Hillyard*	1914	Mrs.R.L.Chambers / *Mrs.D.T.R.Larcombe*	1950	Miss A.L.Brough / *Mrs.W.du Pont*	*1976	Miss C.M.Evert / *Mrs.R.A.Cawley*	2001	Miss V.E.S.Williams / *Miss J.Henin*
*1889	Mrs.G.W.Hillyard / *Miss H.G.B.Rice*	1919	Miss S.R.F.Lenglen / *Mrs.R.L.Chambers*	1951	Miss D.J.Hart / *Miss S.J.Fry*	1977	Miss S.V.Wade / *Miss B.F.Stove*	2002	Miss S.J.Williams / *Miss V.E.S.Williams*
*1890	Miss H.G.B.Rice / *Miss M.Jacks*	1920	Miss S.R.F.Lenglen / *Mrs.R.L.Chambers*	1952	Miss M.C.Connolly / *Miss A.L.Brough*	1978	Miss M.Navratilova / *Miss C.M.Evert*	2003	Miss S.J.Williams / *Miss V.E.S.Williams*
*1891	Miss C.Dod / *Mrs.G.W.Hillyard*	1921	Miss S.R.F.Lenglen / *Miss E.M.Ryan*	1953	Miss M.C.Connolly / *Miss D.J.Hart*	1979	Miss M.Navratilova / *Mrs.J.M.Lloyd*	2004	Miss M.Sharapova / *Miss S.J.Williams*
1892	Miss C.Dod / *Mrs.G.W.Hillyard*	†1922	Miss S.R.F.Lenglen / *Mrs.F.I.Mallory*	1954	Miss M.C.Connolly / *Miss A.L.Brough*	1980	Mrs.R.A.Cawley / *Mrs.J.M.Lloyd*	2005	Miss V.E.S.Williams / *Miss L.A.Davenport*
1893	Miss C.Dod / *Mrs.G.W.Hillyard*	1923	Miss S.R.F.Lenglen / *Miss K.McKane*	*1955	Miss A.L.Brough / *Mrs.J.G.Fleitz*	*1981	Mrs.J.M.Lloyd / *Miss H.Mandlikova*	2006	Miss A.Mauresmo / *Mrs J.Henin-Hardenne*
*1894	Mrs.G.W.Hillyard / *Miss E.L.Austin*	1924	Miss K.McKane / *Miss H.N.Wills*	1956	Miss S.J.Fry / *Miss A.Buxton*	1982	Miss M.Navratilova / *Mrs.J.M.Lloyd*	2007	Miss V.E.S.Williams / *Miss M.S.Bartoli*
*1895	Miss C.R.Cooper / *Miss H.Jackson*	1925	Miss S.R.F.Lenglen / *Miss J.C.Fry*	*1957	Miss A.Gibson / *Miss D.R.Hard*	1983	Miss M.Navratilova / *Miss A.Jaeger*	2008	Miss V.E.S.Williams / *Miss S.J.Williams*
1896	Miss C.R.Cooper / *Mrs.W.H.Pickering*	1926	Mrs.L.A.Godfree / *Miss E.M.de Alvarez*	1958	Miss A.Gibson / *Miss F.A.M.Mortimer*	1984	Miss M.Navratilova / *Mrs.J.M.Lloyd*	2009	Miss S.J.Williams / *Miss V.E.S.Williams*
1897	Mrs.G.W.Hillyard / *Miss C.R.Cooper*	1927	Miss H.Wills / *Miss E.M.de Alvarez*	*1959	Miss M.E.A.Bueno / *Miss D.R.Hard*	1985	Miss M.Navratilova / *Mrs.J.M.Lloyd*	2010	Miss S.J.Williams / *Miss V.Zvonareva*
*1898	Miss C.R.Cooper / *Miss M.L.Martin*	1928	Miss H.N.Wills / *Miss E.M.de Alvarez*	1960	Miss M.E.A.Bueno / *Miss S.Reynolds*	1986	Miss M.Navratilova / *Miss H.Mandlikova*	2011	Miss P.Kvitova / *Miss M.Sharapova*
1899	Mrs.G.W.Hillyard / *Miss C.R.Cooper*	1929	Miss H.N.Wills / *Miss H.H.Jacobs*	*1961	Miss F.A.M.Mortimer / *Miss C.C.Truman*	1987	Miss M.Navratilova / *Miss S.M.Graf*	2012	Miss S.J.Williams / *Miss A.R.Radwanska*
1900	Mrs.G.W.Hillyard / *Miss C.R.Cooper*	1930	Mrs.F.S.Moody / *Miss E.M.Ryan*	1962	Mrs.J.R.Susman / *Mrs.C.Sukova*	1988	Miss S.M.Graf / *Miss M.Navratilova*	2013	Miss M.S.Bartoli / *Miss S.Lisicki*
1901	Mrs.A.Sterry / *Mrs.G.W.Hillyard*	*1931	Miss C.Aussem / *Miss H.Krahwinkel*	*1963	Miss M.Smith / *Miss B.J.Moffitt*	1989	Miss S.M.Graf / *Miss M.Navratilova*	2014	Miss P.Kvitova / *Miss E.C.M.Bouchard*
1902	Miss M.E.Robb / *Mrs.A.Sterry*	*1932	Mrs.F.S.Moody / *Miss H.H.Jacobs*	1964	Miss M.E.A.Bueno / *Miss M.Smith*	1990	Miss M.Navratilova / *Miss Z.L.Garrison*	2015	Miss S.J.Williams / *Miss G.Muguruza*
*1903	Miss D.K.Douglass / *Miss E.W.Thomson*	1933	Mrs.F.S.Moody / *Miss D.E.Round*	1965	Miss M.Smith / *Miss M.E.A.Bueno*	1991	Miss S.M.Graf / *Miss G.B.Sabatini*		
1904	Miss D.K.Douglass / *Mrs.A.Sterry*	*1934	Miss D.E.Round / *Miss H.H.Jacobs*	1966	Mrs.L.W.King / *Miss M.E.A.Bueno*	1992	Miss S.M.Graf / *Miss M.Seles*		
1905	Miss M.G.Sutton / *Miss D.K.Douglass*	1935	Mrs.F.S.Moody / *Miss H.H.Jacobs*	1967	Mrs.L.W.King / *Mrs.P.F.Jones*	1993	Miss S.M.Graf / *Miss J.Novotna*		
1906	Miss D.K.Douglass / *Miss M.G.Sutton*	*1936	Miss H.H.Jacobs / *Miss S.Sperling*	1968	Mrs.L.W.King / *Miss J.A.M.Tegart*	1994	Miss I.C.Martinez / *Miss M.Navratilova*		
1907	Miss M.G.Sutton / *Mrs.R.L.Chambers*	1937	Mrs.D.E.Round / *Miss J.Jedrzejowska*	1969	Mrs.P.F.Jones / *Mrs.L.W.King*	1995	Miss S.M.Graf / *Miss A.I.M.Sanchez Vicario*		
*1908	Mrs.A.Sterry / *Miss A.M.Morton*	*1938	Mrs.F.S.Moody / *Miss H.H.Jacobs*	*1970	Mrs.B.M.Court / *Mrs.L.W.King*	1996	Miss S.M.Graf / *Miss A.I.M.Sanchez Vicario*		
*1909	Miss P.D.H.Boothby / *Miss A.M.Morton*	*1939	Miss A.Marble / *Miss K.E.Stammers*	1971	Miss E.F.Goolagong / *Mrs.B.M.Court*				

GENTLEMEN'S DOUBLES CHAMPIONS & RUNNERS-UP

1879   L.R.Erskine and H.F.Lawford
F.Durant and G.E.Tabor

1880   W.C.Renshaw and J.E.Renshaw
O.E.Woodhouse and C.J.Cole

1881   W.C.Renshaw and J.E.Renshaw
W.J.Down and H.Vaughan

1882   J.T.Hartley and R.T.Richardson
J.G.Horn and C.B.Russell

1883   C.W.Grinstead and C.E.Welldon
C.B.Russell and R.T.Milford

1884   W.C.Renshaw and J.E.Renshaw
E.W.Lewis and E.L.Williams

1885   W.C.Renshaw and J.E.Renshaw
C.E.Farrer and A.J.Stanley

1886   W.C.Renshaw and J.E.Renshaw
C.E.Farrer and A.J.Stanley

1887   P.B.Lyon and
H.W.W.Wilberforce
J.H.Crispe and E.Barratt Smith

1888   W.C.Renshaw and J.E.Renshaw
*P B.Lyon and
H.W.W.Wilberforce*

1889   W.C.Renshaw and J.E.Renshaw
E.W.Lewis and G.W.Hillyard

1890   J.Pim and F.O.Stoker
E.W.Lewis and G.W.Hillyard

1891   W.Baddeley and H.Baddeley
J.Pim and F.O.Stoker

1892   H.S.Barlow and E.W.Lewis
W.Baddeley and H.Baddeley

1893   J.Pim and F.O.Stoker
E.W.Lewis and H.S.Barlow

1894   W.Baddeley and H.Baddeley
H.S.Barlow and C.H.Martin

1895   W.Baddeley and H.Baddeley
E.W.Lewis and W.V.Eaves

1896   W.Baddeley and H.Baddeley
R.F.Doherty and H.A.Nisbet

1897   R.F.Doherty and H.L.Doherty
W.Baddeley and H.Baddeley

1898   R.F.Doherty and H.L .Doherty
H.A.Nisbet and C.Hobart

1899   R.F.Doherty and H.L.Doherty
H.A.Nisbet and C.Hobart

1900   R.F.Doherty and H.L.Doherty
H.R.Barrett and H.A.Nisbet

1901   R.F.Doherty and H.L.Doherty
D.Davis and H.Ward

1902   S.H.Smith and F.L.Riseley
R.F.Doherty and H.L.Doherty

1903   R.F.Doherty and H.L.Doherty
S.H.Smith and F.L.Riseley

1904   R.F.Doherty and H.L.Doherty
S.H.Smith and F.L.Riseley

1905   R.F.Doherty and H.L.Doherty
S.H.Smith and F.L.Riseley

1906   S.H.Smith and F.L.Riseley
R.F.Doherty and H.L.Doherty

1907   N.E.Brookes and A.F.Wilding
B.C.Wright and K.Behr

1908   A.F.Wilding and M.J.G.Ritchie
A.W.Gore and H.R.Barrett

1909   A.W.Gore and H.R.Barrett
S.N.Doust and H.A.Parker

1910   A.F.Wilding and M.J.G.Ritchie
A.W.Gore and H.R.Barrett

1911   M.O.M.Decugis and A.H.Gobert
M.J.G.Ritchie and A.F.Wilding

1912   H.R.Barrett and C.P.Dixon
M.O.Decugis and A.H.Gobert

1913   H.R.Barrett and C.P.Dixon
F.W.Rahe and H.Kleinschroth

1914   N.E.Brookes and A.F.Wilding
H.R.Barrett and C.P.Dixon

1919   R.V.Thomas and P.O.Wood
R.Lycett and R.W.Heath

1920   R.N.Williams and C.S.Garland
A.R.F.Kingscote and J.C.Parke

1921   R.Lycett and M.Woosnam
F.G.Lowe and A.H.Lowe

1922   R.Lycett and J.O.Anderson
G.L.Patterson and P.O.Wood

1923   R.Lycett and L.A.Godfree
*Count M. de Gomar and
E.Flaquer*

1924   F.T.Hunter and V.Richards
*R.N.Williams and
W.M.Washburn*

1925   J.R.Borotra and R.Lacoste
J.F.Hennessey and R.J.Casey

1926   H.J.Cochet and J.Brugnon
V.Richards and H.O.Kinsey

1927   F.T.Hunter and W.T.Tilden
J.Brugnon and H.J.Cochet

1928   H.J.Cochet and J.Brugnon
G.L.Patterson and J.B.Hawkes

1929   W.L.Allison and J.W.Van Ryn
J.C.Gregory and I.G.Collins

1930   W.L.Allison and J.W.Van Ryn
J.T.G.H.Doeg and G.M.Lott

1931   G.M Lott and J.W.Van Ryn
H.J.Cochet and J.Brugnon

1932   J.R.Borotra and J.Brugnon
G.P.Hughes and F.J.Perry

1933   J.R.Borotra and J.Brugnon
R.Nunoi and J.Satoh

1934   G.M.Lott and L.R.Stoefen
J.R.Borotra and J.Brugnon

1935   J.H.Crawford and A.K.Quist
W.L.Allison and J.W.Van Ryn

1936   G.P.Hughes and C.R.D.Tuckey
C.E.Hare and F.H.D.Wilde

1937   J.D.Budge and G.C.Mako
G.P.Hughes and C.R.D.Tuckey

1938   J.D.Budge and G.C.Mako
H.E.O.Henkel and G.von Metaxa

1939   R.L.Riggs and E.T.Cooke
C.E.Hare and F.H.D.Wilde

1946   T.P.Brown and J.A.Kramer
G.E.Brown and D.R.Pails

1947   R.Falkenburg and J.A.Kramer
A.J.Mottram and O.W.T.Sidwell

1948   J.E.Bromwich and F.A.Sedgman
T.P.Brown and G.P.Mulloy

1949   R.A.Gonzales and F.A.Parker
G.P.Mulloy and F.R.Schroeder

1950   J.E.Bromwich and A.K.Quist
G.E.Brown and O.W.T.Sidwell

1951   K.B.McGregor and F.A.Sedgman
J.Drobny and E.W.Sturgess

1952   K.B.McGregor and F.A.Sedgman
E.V.Seixas and E.W.Sturgess

1953   L.A.Hoad and K.R.Rosewall
R.N.Hartwig and M.G.Rose

1954   R.N.Hartwig and M.G.Rose
E.V.Seixas and M.A.Trabert

1955   R.N.Hartwig and L.A.Hoad
N.A.Fraser and K.R.Rosewall

1956   L.A.Hoad and K.R.Rosewall
N.Pietrangeli and O.Sirola

1957   G.P.Mulloy and J.E.Patty
N.A.Fraser and L.A.Hoad

1958   S.V.Davidson and U.C.J.Schmidt
A.J.Cooper and N.A.Fraser

1959   R.S.Emerson and N.A.Fraser
R.G.Laver and R.Mark

1960   R.H.Osuna and R.D.Ralston
M.G.Davies and R.K.Wilson

1961   R.S.Emerson and N.A.Fraser
R.A.J.Hewitt and F.S.Stolle

1962   R.A.J.Hewitt and F.S.Stolle
B.Jovanovic and N.Pilic

1963   R.H.Osuna and A.Palafox
J.C.Barclay and P.Darmon

1964   R.A.J.Hewitt and F.S.Stolle
R.S.Emerson and K.N.Fletcher

1965   J.D.Newcombe and A.D.Roche
K.N.Fletcher and R.A.J.Hewitt

1966   K.N.Fletcher and J.D.Newcombe
W.W.Bowrey and O.K.Davidson

1967   R.A.J.Hewitt and F.D.McMillan
R.S.Emerson and K.N.Fletcher

1968   J.D.Newcombe and A.D.Roche
K.R.Rosewall and F.S.Stolle

1969   J.D.Newcombe and A.D.Roche
T.S.Okker and M.C.Reissen

1970   J.D.Newcombe and A.D.Roche
K.R.Rosewall and F.S.Stolle

1971   R.S.Emerson and R.G.Laver
A.R.Ashe and R.D.Ralston

1972   R.A.J.Hewitt and F.D.McMillan
S.R.Smith and E.J.van Dillen

1973   J.S.Connors and I.Nastase
J.R.Cooper and N.A.Fraser

1974   J.D.Newcombe and A.D.Roche
R.C.Lutz and S.R.Smith

1975   V.K.Gerulaitis and A.Mayer
C.Dowdeswell and A.J.Stone

1976   B.E.Gottfried and R.C.Ramirez
R.L.Case and G.Masters

1977   R.L.Case and G.Masters
J.G.Alexander and P.C.Dent

1978   R.A.J.Hewitt and F.D.McMillan
P.B.Fleming and J.P.McEnroe

1979   P.B.Fleming and J.P.McEnroe
B.E.Gottfried and R.C.Ramirez

1980   P.McNamara and P.F.McNamee
R.C.Lutz and S.R.Smith

1981   P.B.Fleming and J.P.McEnroe
R.C.Lutz and S.R.Smith

1982   P.McNamara and P.F.McNamee
P.B.Fleming and J.P.McEnroe

1983   P.B.Fleming and J.P.McEnroe
T.E.Gullikson and T.R.Gullikson

1984   P.B.Fleming and J.P.McEnroe
P.Cash and P.McNamee

1985   H.P.Guenthardt and B.Taroczy
P.H.Cash and J.B.Fitzgerald

1986   T.K.Nystrom and
M.A.O.Wilander
G.W.Donnelly and P.B.Fleming

1987   K.E.Flach and R.A.Seguso
S.Casal and E.Sanchez

1988   K.E.Flach and R.A.Seguso
J.B.Fitzgerald and A.P.Jarryd

1989   J.B.Fitzgerald and A.P.Jarryd
R.D.Leach and J.R.Pugh

1990   R.D.Leach and J.R.Pugh
P.Aldrich and D.T.Visser

1991   J.B.Fitzgerald and A.P.Jarryd
J.A.Frana and L.Lavalle

1992   J.P.McEnroe and M.D.Stich
J.F.Grabb and R.A.Reneberg

1993   T.A.Woodbridge and
M.R.Woodforde
G.D.Connell and P.J.Galbraith

1994   T.A.Woodbridge and
M.R.Woodforde
G.D.Connell and P.J.Galbraith

1995   T.A.Woodbridge and
M.R.Woodforde
R.D.Leach and S.D.Melville

1996   T.A.Woodbridge and
M.R.Woodforde
B.H.Black and G.D.Connell

1997   T.A.Woodbridge and
M.R.Woodforde
J.F.Eltingh and P.V.N.Haarhuis

1998   J.F.Eltingh and P.V.N.Haarhuis
*T.A.Woodbridge and
M.R.Woodforde*

1999   M.S.Bhupathi and L.A.Paes
P.V.NHaarhuis and J.E.Palmer

2000   T.A.Woodbridge and
M.R.Woodforde
P.V.N.Haarhuis and S.F.Stolle

2001   D.J.Johnson and J.E.Palmer
J.Novak and D.Rikl

2002   J.L.Bjorkman and T.A
Woodbridge
M.S.Knowles and D.M.Nestor

2003   J.L.Bjorkman and T.A
Woodbridge
M.S.Bhupathi and M.N.Mirnyi

2004   J.L.Bjorkman and T.A
Woodbridge
J.Knowle and N.Zimonjic

2005   S.W.I.Huss and W.A.Moodie
R.C.Bryan and M.C.Bryan

2006   R.C.Bryan and M.C.Bryan
F.V.Santoro and N.Zimonjic

2007   A.Clement and M.Llodra
R.C.Bryan and M.C.Bryan

2008   D.M.Nestor and N.Zimonjic
J.L.Bjorkman and K.R.Ullyett

2009   D.M.Nestor and N.Zimonjic
R.C.Bryan and M.C.Bryan

2010   J.Melzer and P.Petzschner
R.S.Lindstedt and H.V.Tecau

2011   R.C.Bryan and M.C.Bryan
R.S.Lindstedt and H.V.Tecau

2012   J.F.Marray and F.L.Nielsen
R.S.Lindstedt and H.V.Tecau

2013   R.C.Bryan and M.C.Bryan
I.Dodig and M.P.D.Melo

2014   V.Pospisil and J.E.Sock
R.C.Bryan and M.C.Bryan

2015   J.J.Rojer and H.Tecau
J.R.Murray and J.Peers

LADIES' DOUBLES CHAMPIONS & RUNNERS-UP

1913	Mrs.R.J.McNair and Miss P.D.H.Boothby *Mrs.A.Sterry and Mrs.R.L.Chambers*	
1914	Miss E.M.Ryan and Miss A.M.Morton *Mrs.D.T.R.Larcombe and Mrs.F.J.Hannam*	
1919	Miss S.R.F.Lenglen and Miss E.M.Ryan *Mrs.R.L.Chambers and Mrs.D.T.R.Larcombe*	
1920	Miss S.R.F.Lenglen and Miss E.M.Ryan *Mrs.R.L.Chambers and Mrs.D.T.R.Larcombe*	
1921	Miss S.R.F.Lenglen and Miss E.M.Ryan *Mrs.A.E.Beamish and Mrs.G.E.Peacock*	
1922	Miss S.R.F.Lenglen and Miss E.M.Ryan *Mrs.A.D.Stocks and Miss K.McKane*	
1923	Miss S.R.F.Lenglen and Miss E.M.Ryan *Miss J.W.Austin and Miss E.L.Colyer*	
1924	Mrs.G.Wightman and Miss H.Wills *Mrs.B.C.Covell and Miss K.McKane*	
1925	Miss S.Lenglen and Miss E.Ryan *Mrs.A.V.Bridge and Mrs.C.G.McIlquham*	
1926	Miss E.M.Ryan and Miss M.K.Browne *Mrs.L.A.Godfree and Miss E.L.Colyer*	
1927	Miss H.N.Wills and Miss E.M.Ryan *Miss E.L.Heine and Mrs.G.E.Peacock*	
1928	Mrs.M.R.Watson and Miss M.A.Saunders *Miss E.H.Harvey and Miss E.Bennett*	
1929	Mrs.M.R.Watson and Mrs.L.R.C.Michell *Mrs.B.C.Covell and Mrs.W.P.Barron*	
1930	Mrs.F.S.Moody and Miss E.M.Ryan *Miss E.A.Cross and Miss S.H.Palfrey*	
1931	Mrs.D.C.Shepherd-Barron and Miss P.E.Mudford *Miss D.E.Metaxa and Miss J.Sigart*	
1932	Miss D.E.Metaxa and Miss J.Sigart *Miss E.M.Ryan and Miss H.H.Jacobs*	
1933	Mrs.R.Mathieu and Miss E.M.Ryan *Miss W.A.James and Miss A.M.Yorke*	
1934	Mrs.R.Mathieu and Miss E.M.Ryan *Mrs.D.B.Andrus and Mrs.C.F.Henrotin*	
1935	Miss W.A.James and Miss K.E.Stammers *Mrs.R.Mathieu and Mrs.S.Sperling*	
1936	Miss W.A.James and Miss K.E.Stammers *Mrs.M.Fabyan and Miss H.H.Jacobs*	
1937	Mrs.R.Mathieu and Miss A.M.Yorke *Mrs.M.R.King and Mrs.J.B.Pittman*	
1938	Mrs.M.Fabyan and Miss A.Marble *Mrs.R.Mathieu and Miss A.M.Yorke*	
1939	Mrs.M.Fabyan and Miss A.Marble *Miss H.H.Jacobs and Miss A.M.Yorke*	
1946	Miss A.L.Brough and Miss M.E.Osborne *Miss P.M.Betz and Miss D.J.Hart*	
1947	Miss D.J.Hart and Mrs.R.B.Todd *Miss A.L.Brough and Miss M.E.Osborne*	
1948	Miss A.L.Brough and Mrs.W.du Pont *Miss D.J.Hart and Mrs.R.B.Todd*	
1949	Miss A.L.Brough and Mrs.W.du Pont *Miss G.Moran and Mrs.R.B.Todd*	
1950	Miss A.L.Brough and Mrs.W.du Pont *Miss S.J.Fry and Miss D.J.Hart*	
1951	Miss S.J.Fry and Miss D.J.Hart *Miss A.L.Brough and Mrs.W.du Pont*	
1952	Miss S.J.Fry and Miss D.J.Hart *Miss A.L.Brough and Miss M.C.Connolly*	
1953	Miss S.J.Fry and Miss D.J.Hart *Miss M.C.Connolly and Miss J.A.Sampson*	
1954	Miss A.L.Brough and Mrs.W.du Pont *Miss S.J.Fry and Miss D.J.Hart*	
1955	Miss F.A.Mortimer and Miss J.A.Shilcock *Miss S.J.Bloomer and Miss P.E.Ward*	
1956	Miss A.Buxton and Miss A.Gibson *Miss E.F.Muller and Miss D.G.Seeney*	
1957	Miss A.Gibson and Miss D.R.Hard *Mrs.K.Hawton and Mrs.M.N.Long*	
1958	Miss M.E.A.Bueno and Miss A.Gibson *Mrs.W.du Pont and Miss M.Varner*	
1959	Miss J.M.Arth and Miss D.R.Hard *Mrs.J.G.Fleitz and Miss C.C.Truman*	
1960	Miss M.E.A.Bueno and Miss D.R.Hard *Miss S.Reynolds and Miss R.Schuurman*	
1961	Miss K.J.Hantze and Miss B.J.Moffitt *Miss J.P.Lehane and Miss M.Smith*	
1962	Miss B.J.Moffitt and Mrs.J.R.Susman *Mrs.L.E.G.Price and Miss R.Schuurman*	
1963	Miss M.E.A.Bueno and Miss D.R.Hard *Miss R.A.Ebbern and Miss M.Smith*	
1964	Miss M.Smith and Miss L.R.Turner *Miss B.J.Moffitt and Mrs.J.R.Susman*	
1965	Miss M.E.A.Bueno and Miss B.J.Moffitt *Miss F.G.Durr and Miss J.P.Lieffrig*	
1966	Miss M.E.A.Bueno and Miss N.A.Richey *Miss M.Smith and Miss J.A.M.Tegart*	
1967	Miss R.Casals and Mrs.L.W.King *Miss M.E.A.Bueno and Miss N.A.Richey*	
1968	Miss R.Casals and Mrs.L.W.King *Miss F.G.Durr and Mrs.P.F.Jones*	
1969	Mrs.B.M.Court and Miss J.A.M.Tegart *Miss P.S.A.Hogan and Miss M.Michel*	
1970	Miss R.Casals and Mrs.L.W.King *Miss F.G.Durr and Miss S.V.Wade*	
1971	Miss R.Casals and Mrs.L.W.King *Mrs.B.M.Court and Miss E.F.Goolagong*	
1972	Mrs.L.W.King and Miss B.F.Stove *Mrs.D.E.Dalton and Miss F.G.Durr*	
1973	Miss R.Casals and Mrs.L.W.King *Miss F.G.Durr and Miss B.F.Stove*	
1974	Miss E.F.Goolagong and Miss M.Michel *Miss H.F.Gourlay and Miss K.M.Krantzcke*	
1975	Miss A.K.Kiyomura and Miss K.Sawamatsu *Miss F.G.Durr and Miss B.F.Stove*	
1976	Miss C.M.Evert and Miss M.Navratilova *Mrs.L.W.King and Miss B.F.Stove*	
1977	Mrs.R.L.Cawley and Miss J.C.Russell *Miss M.Navratilova and Miss B.F.Stove*	
1978	Mrs.G.E.Reid and Miss W.M.Turnbull *Miss M.Jausovec and Miss V.Ruzici*	
1979	Mrs.L.W.King and Miss M.Navratilova *Miss B.F.Stove and Miss W.M.Turnbull*	
1980	Miss K.Jordan and Miss A.E.Smith *Miss R.Casals and Miss W.M.Turnbull*	
1981	Miss M.Navratilova and Miss P.H.Shriver *Miss K.Jordan and Miss A.E.Smith*	
1982	Miss M.Navratilova and Miss P.H.Shriver *Miss K.Jordan and Miss A.E.Smith*	
1983	Miss M.Navratilova and Miss P.H.Shriver *Miss R.Casals and Miss W.M.Turnbull*	
1984	Miss M.Navratilova and Miss P.H.Shriver *Miss K.Jordan and Miss A.E.Smith*	
1985	Miss K.Jordan and Mrs.P.D.Smylie *Miss M.Navratilova and Miss P.H.Shriver*	
1986	Miss M.Navratilova and Miss P.H.Shriver *Miss H.Mandlikova and Miss W.M.Turnbull*	
1987	Miss C.G.Kohde-Kilsch and Miss H.Sukova *Miss H.E.Nagelsen and Mrs.P.D.Smylie*	
1988	Miss S.M.Graf and Miss G.B.Sabatini *Miss L.I.Savchenko and Miss N.M.Zvereva*	
1989	Miss J.Novotna and Miss H.Sukova *Miss L.I.Savchenko and Miss N.M.Zvereva*	
1990	Miss J.Novotna and Miss H.Sukova *Miss K.Jordan and Mrs.P.D.Smylie*	
1991	Miss L.I.Savchenko and Miss N.M.Zvereva *Miss B.C.Fernandez and Miss J.Novotna*	
1992	Miss B.C.Fernandez and Miss N.M.Zvereva *Miss J.Novotna and Mrs.A.Neiland*	
1993	Miss B.C.Fernandez and Miss N.M.Zvereva *Mrs.A.Neiland and Miss J.Novotna*	
1994	Miss B.C.Fernandez and Miss N.M.Zvereva *Miss J.Novotna and Miss A.I.M.Sanchez Vicario*	
1995	Miss J.Novotna and Miss A.I.M.Sanchez Vicario *Miss B.C.Fernandez and Miss N.M.Zvereva*	
1996	Miss M.Hingis and Miss H.Sukova *Miss M.J.McGrath and Mrs.A.Neiland*	
1997	Miss B.C.Fernandez and Miss N.M.Zvereva *Miss N.J.Arendt and Miss M.M.Bollegraf*	
1998	Miss M.Hingis and Miss J.Novotna *Miss L.A.Davenport and Miss N.M.Zvereva*	
1999	Miss L.A.Davenport and Miss C.M.Morariu *Miss M.de Swardt and Miss E.Tatarkova*	
2000	Miss S.J.Williams and Miss V.E.S.Williams *Mrs.A.Decugis and Miss A.Sugiyama*	
2001	Miss L.M.Raymond and Miss R.P.Stubbs *Miss K.Clijsters and Miss A.Sugiyama*	
2002	Miss S.J.Williams and Miss V.E.S.Williams *Miss V.Ruano Pascual and Miss P.L.Suarez*	
2003	Miss K.Clijsters and Miss A.Sugiyama *Miss V.Ruano Pascual and Miss P.L.Suarez*	
2004	Miss C.C.Black and Miss R.P.Stubbs *Mrs.A.Huber and Miss A.Sugiyama*	
2005	Miss C.C.Black and Mrs.A.Huber *Miss S.Kuznetsova and Miss A.Muresmo*	
2006	Miss Z.Yan and Miss J.Zheng *Miss V.Ruano Pascual and Miss P.L.Suarez*	
2007	Miss C.C.Black and Mrs.A.Huber *Miss K.Srebotnik and Miss A.Sugiyama*	
2008	Miss S.J.Williams and Miss V.E.S.Williams *Miss L.M.Raymond and Miss S.J.Stosur*	
2009	Miss S.J.Williams and Miss V.E.S.Williams *Miss S.J.Stosur and Miss R.P.Stubbs*	
2010	Miss V.King and Miss Y.V.Shvedova *Miss E.S.Vesnina and Miss V.Zvonareva*	
2011	Miss K.Peschke and Miss K.Srebotnik *Miss S.Lisicki and Miss S.J.Stosur*	
2012	Miss S.J.Williams and Miss V.E.S.Williams *Miss A.Hlavackova and Miss L.Hradecka*	
2013	Miss S-W.Hsieh and Miss S.Peng *Miss A.Barty and Miss C.Dellacqua*	
2014	Miss S.Errani and Miss R.Vinci *Miss T.Babos and Miss K.Mladenovic*	
2015	Miss M.Hingis and Miss S.Mirza *Miss E.Makarova and Miss E.S.Vesnina*	

MIXED DOUBLES CHAMPIONS & RUNNERS-UP

1913 H.Crisp and Mrs.C.O.Tuckey
J.C.Parke and Mrs.D.T.R.Larcombe

1914 J.C.Parke and Mrs.D.T.R.Larcombe
A.F.Wilding and Miss M.Broquedis

1919 R.Lycett and Miss E.M.Ryan
A.D.Prebble and Mrs.R.L.Chambers

1920 G.L.Patterson and Miss S.R.F.Lenglen
R.Lycett and Miss E.M.Ryan

1921 R.Lycett and Miss E.M.Ryan
M.Woosnam and Miss P.L.Howkins

1922 P.O.Wood and Miss S.R.F.Lenglen
R.Lycett and Miss E.M.Ryan

1923 R.Lycett and Miss E.M.Ryan
L.S.Deane and Mrs.W.P.Barron

1924 J.B.Gilbert and Miss K.McKane
L.A.Godfree and Mrs.W.P.Barron

1925 J.Borotra and Miss S.R.F.Lenglen
U.L.de Morpurgo and Miss E.M.Ryan

1926 L.A.Godfree and Mrs.L.A.Godfree
H.O.Kinsey and Miss M.K.Browne

1927 F.T.Hunter and Miss E.M.Ryan
L.A.Godfree and Mrs.L.A.Godfree

1928 P.D.B.Spence and Miss E.M.Ryan
J.H.Crawford and Miss D.J.Akhurst

1929 F.T.Hunter and Miss H.N.Wills
I.G.Collins and Miss J.C.Fry

1930 J.H.Crawford and Miss E.M.Ryan
D.D.Prenn and Miss H.Krahwinkel

1931 G.M.Lott and Mrs.L.A.Harper
I.G.Collins and Miss J.C.Ridley

1932 E.G.Maier and Miss E.M.Ryan
H.C.Hopman and Miss J.Sigart

1933 G.von Cramm and Miss H.Krahwinkel
N.G.Farquharson and Miss G.M.Heeley

1934 R.Miki and Miss D.E.Round
H.W.Austin and Mrs.W.P.Barron

1935 F.J.Perry and Miss D.E.Round
H.C.Hopman and Mrs.H.C.Hopman

1936 F.J.Perry and Miss D.E.Round
J.D.Budge and Mrs.M.Fabyan

1937 J.D.Budge and Miss A.Marble
Y.F.M.Petra and Mrs.R.Mathieu

1938 J.D.Budge and Miss A.Marble
H.E.O.Henkel and Mrs.M.Fabyan

1939 R.L.Riggs and Miss A.Marble
F.H.D.Wilde and Miss N.B.Brown

1946 T.P.Brown and Miss A.L.Brough
G.E.Brown and Miss D.M.Bundy

1947 J.E.Bromwich and Miss A.L.Brough
C.F.Long and Mrs.G.F.Bolton

1948 J.E.Bromwich and Miss A.L.Brough
F.A.Sedgman and Miss D.J.Hart

1949 E.W.Sturgess and Mrs.R.A.Summers
J.E.Bromwich and Miss A.L.Brough

1950 E.W.Sturgess and Miss A.L.Brough
G.E.Brown and Mrs.R.B.Todd

1951 F.A.Sedgman and Miss D.J.Hart
M.G.Rose and Mrs.G.F.Bolton

1952 F.A.Sedgman and Miss D.J.Hart
E.J.Morea and Mrs.M.N.Long

1953 E.V.Seixas and Miss D.J.Hart
E.J.Morea and Miss S.J.Fry

1954 E.V.Seixas and Miss D.J.Hart
K.R.Rosewall and Mrs.W.du Pont

1955 E.V.Seixas and Miss D.J.Hart
E.J.Morea and Miss A.L.Brough

1956 E.V.Seixas and Miss S.J.Fry
G.P.Mulloy and Miss A.Gibson

1957 M.G.Rose and Miss D.R.Hard
N.A.Fraser and Miss A.Gibson

1958 R.N.Howe and Miss L.Coghlan
K.Nielsen and Miss A.Gibson

1959 R.G.Laver and Miss D.R.Hard
N.A.Fraser and Miss M.E.A.Bueno

1960 R.G.Laver and Miss D.R.Hard
R.N.Howe and Miss M.E.A.Bueno

1961 F.S.Stolle and Miss L.R.Turner
R.N.Howe and Miss E.Buding

1962 N.A.Fraser and Mrs.W.du Pont
R.D.Ralston and Miss A.S.Haydon

1963 K.N.Fletcher and Miss M.Smith
R.A.J.Hewitt and Miss D.R.Hard

1964 F.S.Stolle and Miss L.R.Turner
K.N.Fletcher and Miss M.Smith

1965 K.N.Fletcher and Miss M.Smith
A.D.Roche and Miss J.A.M.Tegart

1966 K.N.Fletcher and Miss M.Smith
R.D.Ralston amd Mrs.L.W.King

1967 O.K.Davidson and Mrs.L.W.King
K.N.Fletcher and Miss M.E.A.Bueno

1968 K.N.Fletcher and Mrs.B.M.Court
A.Metreveli and Miss O.V.Morozova

1969 F.S.Stolle and Mrs.P.F.Jones
A.D.Roche and Miss J.A.M.Tegart

1970 I.Nastase and Miss R.Casals
A.Metreveli and Miss O.V.Morozova

1971 O.K.Davidson and Mrs.L.W.King
M.C.Riessen and Mrs.B.M.Court

1972 I.Nastase and Miss R.Casals
K.G.Warwick and Miss E.F.Goolagong

1973 O.K.Davidson and Mrs.L.W.King
R.C.Ramirez and Miss J.S.Newberry

1974 O.K.Davidson and Mrs.L.W.King
M.J.Farrell and Miss L.J.Charles

1975 M.C.Riessen and Mrs.B.M.Court
A.J.Stone and Miss B.F.Stove

1976 A.D.Roche and Miss F.G.Durr
R.L.Stockton and Miss R.Casals

1977 R.A.J.Hewitt and Miss G.R.Stevens
F.D.McMillan and Miss B.F.Stove

1978 F.D.McMillan and Miss B.F.Stove
R.O.Ruffels and Mrs.L.W.King

1979 R.A.J.Hewitt and Miss G.R.Stevens
F.D.McMillan and Miss B.F.Stove

1980 J.R.Austin and Miss T.A.Austin
M.R.Edmondson and Miss D.L.Fromholtz

1981 F.D.McMillan and Miss B.F.Stove
J.R.Austin and Miss T.A.Austin

1982 K.M.Curren and Miss A.E.Smith
J.M.Lloyd and Miss W.M.Turnbull

1983 J.M.Lloyd and Miss W.M.Turnbull
S.B.Denton and Mrs.L.W.King

1984 J.M.Lloyd and Miss W.M.Turnbull
S.B.Denton and Miss K.Jordan

1985 P.F.McNamee and Miss M.Navratilova
J.B.Fitzgerald and Mrs.P.D.Smylie

1986 K.E.Flach and Miss K.Jordan
H.P.Guenthardt and Miss M.Navratilova

1987 M.J.Bates and Miss J.M.Durie
D.A.Cahill and Miss N.A-L.Provis

1988 S.E.Stewart and Miss Z.L.Garrison
K.L.Jones and Mrs.S.W.Magers

1989 J.R.Pugh and Miss J.Novotna
M.Kratzmann and Miss J.M.Byrne

1990 R.D.Leach and Miss Z.L.Garrison
J.B.Fitzgerald and Mrs.P.D.Smylie

1991 J.B.Fitzgerald and Mrs.P.D.Smylie
J.R.Pugh and Miss N.M.Zvereva

1992 C.Suk and Mrs.A.Neiland
J.F.Eltingh and Miss M.J.M.M.Oremans

1993 M.R.Woodforde and Miss M.Navratilova
T.J.C.M.Nijssen and Miss M.M.Bollegraf

1994 T.A.Woodbridge and Miss H.Sukova
T.J.Middleton and Miss L.M.McNeil

1995 J.A.Stark and Miss M.Navratilova
C.Suk and Miss B.C.Fernandez

1996 C.Suk and Miss H.Sukova
M.R.Woodforde and Mrs.A.Neiland

1997 C.Suk and Miss H.Sukova
A.Olhovskiy and Mrs.A.Neiland

1998 M.N.Mirnyi and Miss S.J.Williams
M.S.Bhupathi and Miss M.Lucic

1999 L.A.Paes and Miss L.M.Raymond
J.L.Bjorkman and Miss A.S.Kournikova

2000 D.J.Johnson and Miss K.Y.Po
L.G.Hewitt and Miss K.Clijsters

2001 L.Friedl and Miss D.Hantuchova
M.C.Bryan and Mrs.A.Huber

2002 M.S.Bhupathi and Miss E.A.Likhovtseva
K.R.Ullyett and Miss D.Hantuchova

2003 L.A.Paes and Miss M.Navratilova
A.Ram and Miss A.Rodionova

2004 W.Black and Miss C.C.Black
T.A.Woodbridge and Miss A.H.Molik

2005 M.S.Bhupathi and Miss M.C.Pierce
P.Hanley and Miss T.Perebiynis

2006 A.Ram and Miss V.Zvonareva
R.C.Bryan and Miss V.E.S.Williams

2007 J.R.Murray and Miss J.Jankovic
J.L.Bjorkman and Miss A.H.Molik

2008 R.C.Bryan and Miss S.J.Stosur
M.C.Bryan and Miss K.Srebotnik

2009 M.S.Knowles and Miss A-L.Groenefeld
L.A.Paes and Miss C.C.Black

2010 L.A.Paes and Miss C.C.Black
W.A.Moodie and Miss L.M.Raymond

2011 J.Melzer and Miss I.Benesova
M.S.Bhupathi and Miss E.S.Vesnina

2012 M.Bryan and Miss L.M.Raymond
L.A.Paes and Miss E.S.Vesnina

2013 D.M.Nestor and Miss K.Mladenovic
B.Soares and Miss L.M.Raymond

2014 N.Zimonjic and Miss S.Stosur
M.N.Mirnyi and Miss H.Chan

2015 L.A.Paes and Miss M.Hingis
A.Peya and Miss T.Babos

BOYS' SINGLES

1947	K.Nielsen *S.V.Davidson*	1965	V.Korotkov *G.Goven*
1948	S.O.Stockenberg *D.Vad*	1966	V.Korotkov *B.E.Fairlie*
1949	S.O.Stockenberg *J.A.T.Horn*	1967	M.Orantes *M.S.Estep*
1950	J.A.T.Horn *K.Mobarek*	1968	J.G.Alexander *J.Thamin*

1947 K.Nielsen
S.V.Davidson
1948 S.O.Stockenberg
D.Vad
1949 S.O.Stockenberg
J.A.T.Horn
1950 J.A.T.Horn
K.Mobarek
1951 J.Kupferburger
K.Mobarek
1952 R.K.Wilson
T.T.Fancutt
1953 W.A.Knight
R.Krishnan
1954 R.Krishnan
A.J.Cooper
1955 M.P.Hann
J.E.Lundquist
1956 R.E.Holmberg
R.G.Laver
1957 J.I.Tattersall
I.Ribeiro
1958 E.H.Buchholz
P.J.Lall
1959 T.Lejus
R.W.Barnes
1960 A.R.Mandelstam
J.Mukerjea
1961 C.E.Graebner
E.Blanke
1962 S.J.Matthews
A.Metreveli
1963 N.Kalogeropoulos
I.El Shafei
1964 I.El Shafei
V.Korotkov

1965 V.Korotkov
G.Goven
1966 V.Korotkov
B.E.Fairlie
1967 M.Orantes
M.S.Estep
1968 J.G.Alexander
J.Thamin
1969 B.M.Bertram
J.G.Alexander
1970 B.M.Bertram
F.Gebert
1971 R.I.Kreiss
S.A.Warboys
1972 B.R.Borg
C.J.Mottram
1973 W.W.Martin
C.S.Dowdeswell
1974 W.W.Martin
Ash Amritraj
1975 C.J.Lewis
R.Ycaza
1976 H.P.Guenthardt
P.Elter
1977 V.A.W.Winitsky
T.E.Teltscher
1978 I.Lendl
J.Turpin
1979 R.Krishnan
D.Siegler
1980 T.Tulasne
H.D.Beutel
1981 M.W.Anger
P.H.Cash
1982 P.H.Cash
H.Sundstrom

1983 S.B.Edberg
J.Frawley
1984 M.Kratzmann
S.Kruger
1985 L.Lavalle
E.Velez
1986 E.Velez
J.Sanchez
1987 D.Nargiso
J.R.Stoltenberg
1988 N.Pereira
G.Raoux
1989 L.J.N.Kulti
T.A.Woodbridge
1990 L.A.Paes
M.Ondruska
1991 K.J.T.Enquist
M.Joyce
1992 D.Skoch
B.Dunn
1993 R.Sabau
J.Szymanski
1994 S.M.Humphries
M.A.Philippoussis
1995 O.Mutis
N.Kiefer
1996 V.Voltchkov
I.Ljubicic
1997 W.Whitehouse
D.Elsner
1998 R.Federer
I.Labadze
1999 J.Melzer
K.Pless
2000 N.P.A.Mahut
M.Ancic

2001 R.Valent
G.Muller
2002 T.C.Reid
L.Quahab
2003 F.Mergea
C.Guccione
2004 G.Monfils
M.Kasiri
2005 J.Chardy
R.Haase
2006 T.De Bakker
M.Gawron
2007 D.Young
V.Ignatic
2008 G.Dimitrov
H.Kontinen
2009 A.Kuznetsov
J.Cox
2010 M.Fucsovics
B.Mitchell
2011 L.Saville
L.Broady
2012 F.Peliwo
L.Saville
2013 G.Quinzi
H.Chung
2014 N.Rubin
S.Kozlov
2015 R.Opelka
M.Ymer

BOYS' DOUBLES

1982 P.H.Cash and J.Frawley
R.D.Leach and J.J.Ross
1983 M.Kratzmann and S.Youl
M.Nastase and O. Rahnasto
1984 R.Brown and R.V.Weiss
M.Kratzmann and J.Svensson
1985 A.Moreno and J.Yzaga
P.Korda and C.Suk
1986 T.Carbonell and P.Korda
S.Barr and H.Karrasch
1987 J.Stoltenberg and T.A.Woodbridge
D.Nargiso and E.Rossi
1988 J.R.Stoltenberg and T.A.Woodbridge
D.Rikl and T.Zdrazila
1989 J.E.Palmer and J.A.Stark
J-L.De Jager and W.R.Ferreira
1990 S.Lareau and S.Leblanc
C.Marsh and M.Ondruska
1991 K.Alami and G.Rusedski
J-L.De Jager and A.Medvedev
1992 S.Baldas and S.Draper
M.S.Bhupathi and N.Kirtane
1993 S.Downs and J.Greenhalgh
N.Godwin and G.Williams
1994 B.Ellwood and M.Philippoussis
V.Platenik and R.Schlachter

1995 J.Lee and J.M.Trotman
A.Hernandez and M.Puerta
1996 D.Bracciali and J.Robichaud
D.Roberts and W.Whitehouse
1997 L.Horna and N.Massu
J.Van de Westhuizen
and W.Whitehouse
1998 R.Federer and O.L.P.Rochus
M.Llodra and A.Ram
1999 G.Coria and D.P.Nalbandian
T.Enev and J.Nieminem
2000 D.Coene and K.Vliegen
A.Banks and B.Riby
2001 F.Dancevic and G.Lapentti
B.Echagaray and S.Gonzales
2002 F.Mergea and H.V.Tecau
B.Baker and B.Ram
2003 F.Mergea and H.V.Tecau
A.Feeney and C.Guccione
2004 B.Evans and S.Oudsema
R.Haase and V.Troicki
2005 J.Levine and M.Shabaz
S.Groth and A.Kennaugh
2006 K.Damico and N.Schnugg
M.Klizan and A.Martin

2007 D.Lopez and M.Trevisan
R.Jebavy and M.Klizan
2008 C-P.Hsieh and T-H.Yang
M.Reid and B.Tomic
2009 P-H.Herbert and K.Krawietz
J.Obry and A.Puget
2010 L.Broady and T.Farquharson
L.Burton and G.Morgan
2011 G.Morgan and M.Pavic
O.Golding and J.Vesely
2012 A.Harris and N.Kyrgios
M.Donati and P.Licciardi
2013 T.Kokkinakis and N.Kyrgios
E.Couacaud and S.Napolitano
2014 O.Luz and M.Zormann
S.Kozlov and A.Rublev
2015 N.H.Ly and S.Nagal
R.Opelka and A.Santillan

GIRLS' SINGLES

1947	Miss G.Domken	1965 Miss O.V.Morozova	1983 Miss P.Paradis

1947 Miss G.Domken
Miss B.Wallen
1948 Miss O.Miskova
Miss V.Rigollet
1949 Miss C.Mercelis
Miss J.S.V.Partridge
1950 Miss L.Cornell
Miss A. Winter
1951 Miss L.Cornell
Miss S.Lazzarino
1952 Miss F.J.I.ten Bosch
Miss R.Davar
1953 Miss D.Kilian
Miss V.A.Pitt
1954 Miss V.A.Pitt
Miss C.Monnot
1955 Miss S.M.Armstrong
Miss B.de Chambure
1956 Miss A.S.Haydon
Miss I.Buding
1957 Miss M.G.Arnold
Miss E.Reyes
1958 Miss S.M.Moore
Miss A.Dmitrieva
1959 Miss J.Cross
Miss D.Schuster
1960 Miss K.J.Hantze
Miss L.M Hutchings
1961 Miss G.Baksheeva
Miss K.D.Chabot
1962 Miss G.Baksheeva
Miss E.P.Terry
1963 Miss D.M.Salfati
Miss K.Dening
1964 Miss J.M.Bartkowicz
Miss E.Subirats

1965 Miss O.V.Morozova
Miss R.Giscarfe
1966 Miss B.Lindstrom
Miss J.A.Congdon
1967 Miss J.H.Salome
Miss E.M.Strandberg
1968 Miss K.S.Pigeon
Miss L.E.Hunt
1969 Miss K.Sawamatsu
Miss B.I.Kirk
1970 Miss S.A.Walsh
Miss M.V.Kroshina
1971 Miss M.V.Kroschina
Miss S.H.Minford
1972 Miss I.S.Kloss
Miss G.L.Coles
1973 Miss A.K.Kiyomura
Miss M.Navratilova
1974 Miss M.Jausovec
Miss M.Simionescu
1975 Miss N.Y.Chmyreva
Miss R.Marsikova
1976 Miss N.Y.Chmyreva
Miss M.Kruger
1977 Miss L.Antonoplis
Miss M. Louie
1978 Miss T.A.Austin
Miss H.Mandlikova
1979 Miss M.L.Piatek
Miss A.A.Moulton
1980 Miss D.Freeman
Miss S.J.Leo
1981 Miss Z.L.Garrison
Miss R.R.Uys
1982 Miss C.Tanvier
Miss H.Sukova

1983 Miss P.Paradis
Miss P.Hy
1984 Miss A.N.Croft
Miss E.Reinach
1985 Miss A.Holikova
Miss J.M.Byrne
1986 Miss N.M.Zvereva
Miss L.Meskhi
1987 Miss N.M.Zvereva
Miss J.Halard
1988 Miss B.A.M.Schultz
Miss E.Derly
1989 Miss A.Strnadova
Miss M.J.McGrath
1990 Miss A.Strnadova
Miss K.Sharpe
1991 Miss B.Rittner
Miss E.Makarova
1992 Miss C.R.Rubin
Miss L.Courtois
1993 Miss N.Feber
Miss R.Grande
1994 Miss M.Hingis
Miss M-R.Jeon
1995 Miss A.Olsza
Miss T.Tanasugarn
1996 Miss A.Mauresmo
Miss M.L.Serna
1997 Miss C.C.Black
Miss A.Rippner
1998 Miss K.Srebotnik
Miss K.Clijsters
1999 Miss I.Tulyagnova
Miss L.Krasnoroutskaya
2000 Miss M.E.Salerni
Miss T.Perebiynis

2001 Miss A.Widjaja
Miss D.Safina
2002 Miss V.Douchevina
Miss M.Sharapova
2003 Miss K.Flipkens
Miss A.Tchakvetadze
2004 Miss K.Bondarenko
Miss A.Ivanovic
2005 Miss A.R.Radwanska
Miss T.Paszek
2006 Miss C.Wozniacki
Miss M.Rybarikova
2007 Miss U.Radwanska
Miss M.Brengle
2008 Miss L.M.D.Robson
Miss N.Lertcheewakarn
2009 Miss N.Lertcheewakarn
Miss K.Mladenovic
2010 Miss K.Pliskova
Miss S.Ishizu
2011 Miss A.Barty
Miss I.Khromacheva
2012 Miss E.Bouchard
Miss E.Svitolina
2013 Miss B.Bencic
Miss T.Townsend
2014 Miss J.Ostapenko
Miss K.Schmiedlova
2015 Miss S.Zhuk
Miss A.Blinkova

GIRLS' DOUBLES

1982 Miss E.A.Herr and Miss P.Barg
Miss B.S.Gerken and Miss G.A.Rush
1983 Miss P.A.Fendick and Miss P.Hy
Miss C.Anderholm and Miss H.Olsson
1984 Miss C.Kuhlman and Miss S.C.Rehe
Miss V.Milvidskaya and Miss L.I.Savchenko
1985 Miss L.Field and Miss J.G.Thompson
Miss E.Reinach and Miss J.A.Richardson
1986 Miss M.Jaggard and Miss L.O'Neill
Miss L.Meskhi and Miss N.M.Zvereva
1987 Miss N.Medvedeva and Miss N.M.Zvereva
Miss I.S.Kim and Miss P.M.Moreno
1988 Miss J.A.Faull and Miss R.McQuillan
Miss A.Dechaume and Miss E.Derly
1989 Miss J.M.Capriati and Miss M.J.McGrath
Miss A.Strnadova and Miss E.Sviglerova
1990 Miss K.Habsudova and Miss A.Strnadova
Miss N.J.Pratt and Miss K.Sharpe
1991 Miss C.Barclay and Miss L.Zaltz
Miss J.Limmer and Miss A.Woolcock
1992 Miss M.Avotins and Miss L.McShea
Miss P.Nelson and Miss J.Steven
1993 Miss L.Courtois and Miss N.Feber
Miss H.Mochizuki and Miss Y.Yoshida

1994 Miss E.De Villiers and Miss E.E.Jelfs
Miss C.M.Morariu and Miss L.Varmuzova
1995 Miss C.C.Black and Miss A.Olsza
Miss T.Musgrove and Miss J. Richardson
1996 Miss O.Barabanschikova and Miss A.Mauresmo
Miss L.Osterloh and Miss S.Reeves
1997 Miss C.C.Black and Miss I.Selyutina
Miss M.Matevzic and Miss K.Srebotnik
1998 Miss E.Dyrberg and Miss J.Kostanic
Miss P.Rampre and Miss I.Tulyaganova
1999 Miss D.Bedanova and Miss M.E.Salerni
Miss T.Perebiynis and Miss I.Tulyaganova
2000 Miss I.Gaspar and Miss T.Perebiynis
Miss D.Bedanova and Miss M.E.Salerni
2001 Miss G.Dulko and Miss A.Harkleroad
Miss C.Horiatopoulos and Miss B.Mattek
2002 Miss E.Clijsters and Miss B.Strycova
Miss A.Baker and Miss A-L.Groenfeld
2003 Miss A.Kleybanova and Miss S.Mirza
Miss K.Bohmova and Miss M.Krajicek
2004 Miss V.A.Azarenka and Miss V.Havartsova
Miss M.Erakovic and Miss M.Niculescu

2005 Miss V.A.Azarenka and Miss A.Szavay
Miss M.Erakovic and Miss M.Niculescu
2006 Miss A.Kleybanova and Miss A.Pavlyuchenkova
Miss K.Antoniychuk and Miss A.Dulgheru
2007 Miss A.Pavlyuchenkova and Miss U.Radwanska
Miss M.Doi and Miss K.Nara
2008 Miss P.Hercog and Miss J.Moore
Miss I.Holland and Miss S.Peers
2009 Miss N.Lertcheewakarn and Miss S.Peers
Miss K.Mladenovic and Miss S.Njiric
2010 Miss T.Babos and Miss S.Stephens
Miss I.Khromacheva and Miss E.Svitolina
2011 Miss E.Bouchard and Miss G.Min
Miss D.Schuurs and Miss H.C. Tang
2012 Miss E.Bouchard and Miss T.Townsend
Miss B.Bencic and Miss A.Konjuh
2013 Miss B.Krejcikova and Miss K.Siniakova
Miss A.Kalinina and Miss I.Shymanovich
2014 Miss T.Grende and Miss Q.Ye
Miss M.Bouzkova and Miss D.Galfi
2015 Miss D.Galfi and Miss F.Stollar
Miss V.Lapko and Miss T.Mihalikova

PICTURE OF THE CHAMPIONSHIPS 2015

Novak Djokovic in dramatic full flight during his semi-final victory
over Richard Gasquet on Centre Court

Photographer

Jed Leicester/AELTC